HOW TO WIN A LAWSUIT WITHOUT HIRING A LAWYER

By Attorney David C. Grossack

Table of Contents

Chapter 1

Winning Your Lawsuit Without A Lawyer

Every day, thousands of people across this country go to court without a lawyer. This is called "pro-se" (for one's self in Latin). Pro-se cases range from the simple dry-cleaning or auto repair dispute filed in a small claims court to cases filed in federal court for police misconduct and other civil rights violations.

The decision to begin a lawsuit without a lawyer is rarely taken lightly. People are often forced to represent themselves pro-se because they have a case that no lawyer is interested in or the proposed financial arrangements were too severe. When lawyers charge in the range of \$175.00-\$250.00 per hour, and the average American earns \$15.00 per hour, legal bills can become devastating to many of us.

Still others have grown so suspicious of the legal profession that they insist on legal self-help.

Despite the large numbers of pro-se litigants, conventional thinking seems to be that lawyers are necessary in all but the very simplest of cases.

Is this thinking accurate?

Experience indicates that a person with a high school education can be quite effective in court without a lawyer.

Effectiveness often seems to be greatly influenced by:

(a) how strong the case is.
(b) how disciplined and determined the pro-se party is. (For example, some excellent pro-se work comes out of jail, where time and motivation are abundant.)

A man in Pembroke, Massachusetts recently won \$200,000.00 in a case he tried pro-se in front of a federal jury for false arrest. He was imprisoned for videotaping a public municipal meeting.

The movie *Gideon's Trumpet* brought to public attention the efforts of the plaintiff in Gideon v. Wainwright, a criminal appeal originally filed pro-se by a prison inmate. The case was ultimately taken on by a lawyer and taken to the U.S. Supreme Court, which ruled that the right to counsel for indigent criminal defendants facing potential loss of liberty was a fundamental, constitutional right rooted in the Sixth Amendment.

Webster Bivens, a pro-se litigant, made new civil rights law when he sued for an illegal search and seizure, ending a long tradition of virtual immunity for federal agents.

The successful pro-se litigant must remember a few basic lessons before even starting a lawsuit.

I. THERE ARE TWO KINDS OF LAW: SUBSTANTIVE LAW AND PROCEDURAL LAW.

Substantive law governs how a case is going to be decided.

Procedural law governs the pleading and evidentiary path the courts will travel to reach their ultimate decision.

Both substantive law and procedural law vary from state to state and court to court.

Know the procedural rules of the court you are in. These are available in the State and Federal statute books. The Federal Rules of Civil Procedure can be ordered from the Government Printing Office, Washington, DC.

II. CHANCES ARE THE CASE YOU HAVE HAS BEEN HEARD BEFORE WITH A SIMILAR LEGAL AND FACTUAL BASIS, AND ALL OF THE PLEADINGS ARE IN A CLERK'S OFFICE WAITING FOR YOU TO COPY.

Those cases are a matter of public record and are not copyrighted.

Using the law library, find a case similar to yours, track down the pleadings, and adapt them to your case. In the volumes that report cases, you will find the name of the court, the docket number and even the names of the lawyers.

III. BECOME A WIZARD AT LEGAL RESEARCH.

Knowing how to use the law library is vital. Knowing which books are related to your case is not easy when you are new. Many libraries have books and videotapes on the subject. A longtime favorite book is Jacobstein & Murphy's Fundamentals of Legal Research. A great videotape is Commando Legal Research. Careful use of the Internet can turn up valuable legal research as well.

IV. GATHER EVIDENCE YOU CAN USE.

Marshall all of the documents, such as contracts, receipts, letters and tangible items that may be helpful to winning your case and organize them in a filing system making them quickly retrievable at a hearing. Bring copies for the opposing side and yourself, with the original going to the court.
Determine what your missing evidentiary gaps are and learn how to use subpoenas and discovery rules to get that necessary "smoking gun."

Don't forget about the Freedom of Information Act and its State equivalents. Learn about as many governmental agencies, departments and bureaus as you have time to.

They often have records and documents that fit into a puzzle sooner or later.

V. USE LAWYERS OR LAW STUDENTS AS COACHES.

If you have a problem, consider using a lawyer or law student as a coach to help with the problem.

VI. USE A LEGAL DICTIONARY AND LEGAL ENCYCLOPEDIA TO LEARN BASIC LEGAL CONCEPTS.

Black's Law Dictionary is a valuable tool. American Jurisprudence and Corpus Juris are also extremely valuable in explaining law and giving research sources.

If your pleadings are not perfect, don't panic. Federal judges have set forth a doctrine that instructs courts to give some latitude to pro-se parties when they make pleading mistakes. (Picking v. Penn Railway, 151 F2d 240)

The road to familiarity with law and legal methods is not going to be easy to travel. It is necessary to have patience and a high tolerance to frustration. But the rewards are valuable. In many ways, knowing the legal system is a form of "survivalist" knowledge, especially in a litigious society as is ours.

Businessmen, professionals, working people, consumers, taxpayers, retirees, the disabled, all the rich and the poor all have specialized legal needs. Getting what you want out of government and the courts, and staying out of trouble, are that much closer to reach when you know how to stand up for your rights on your own.

Chapter 2

How to Organize a Lawsuit

Fourteen Steps to Justice!

1. Analyze the fact pattern. What kind of case do you have and what kind of remedy do you want?

2. Go to the law library and find a precedent. Track down pleadings from clerk's office. Also check form books. Make sure you have a cause of action which is well grounded in both facts and law.

3. Formulate model pleadings.

4. Serve process.

5. Prepare for any dispositive motions. Anticipate motion for summary judgement and plan rebuttal.

6. Serve discovery.

7. Consider plaintiff's motion for summary judgement, on liability alone if not damages.

8. Plan trial, prepare pre trial memo.

9. Locate assets, explore possibility of pretrial attachments.

10. Plan trial through questions and answers for anticipated witnesses. Issue subpoenas.

11. Organize exhibits.

12. Jury instructions.

13. Request execution on judgement.

14. Levy on assets or institute supplementary proceedings.

Steps to Justice

1. Categorize the Action

The first thing you have to do when faced with a legal action is to decide what category of a legal problem it is.

If a neighbor is dumping garbage on your front lawn, you have a number of ways you can proceed. A civil lawsuit for money damages based on the common law actions of nuisance and trespass is one possibility.

Criminal complaints brought by civilian parties are accepted in Massachusetts, and a criminal complaint for illegal dumping of garbage, or whatever the local municipal ordinance is, is a possible course of action as is a criminal complaint for trespass.

It may be a civil rights case if the motive for wrongful conduct was to harass on the basis of one's ethnicity, race or sexual preference.

Sometimes these matters can be handled by governmental agencies or police without a lawyer ever being involved.

Sometimes you may want money damages or sometimes you may want what is called "injunctive relief," a court order enjoining the neighbor from doing it again under the penalty of contempt.

Some readers may decide they want to sue the neighbor to obtain adequate compensation, and do not want to pay a lawyer to do it.

Use of small claims procedures are an excellent way to handle a "neighbor problem." Damages are often limited, and there is no jury trial and no discovery (formal exchanges of answers to written questions called "interrogatories," depositions, document requests and so forth) but this is probably not necessary in this kind of minor problem.

More sophisticated approaches are also possible to this situation.

For example, the law recognized an action called "intentional infliction of emotional distress." When conduct is intolerable and outrageous to a degree that no civilized person will be able to endure it, a claim for intentional infliction of emotional distress may be appropriate.

Thus you can see that there are a number of alternative directions available to resolving this controversy.

Once you have found the path you wish to pursue in your redress of grievances, your next step is to organize your thinking in such a manner as to prepare for war.

Using the Law Library

2. Beginning Your Research

Do not be overwhelmed by the thousands of volumes in the library. If you know what information you are looking for, once you know how the law library is organized, the task is much easier.

You might want to keep the following things in mind:

There are approximately eight million municipal county, state, and federal laws, rules regulations promulgated by government bodies, including legislatures, administrative agencies, municipal governments, boards, county commissions, authorities, departments and other entities.

There are probably as many court decisions which interpret these laws in the context of various fact patterns. State courts and federal court on the various levels, appellate courts, county courts, probate courts all make decisions. If the decisions were not made based on a statute or regulation, they were most likely made on the basis of common law, i.e. generally recognized principles of jurisprudence originating in the law of the Anglo Saxons from whom our own system is derived. Common law, however, changes from the body of each new court decision handed down each day. These decisions are based on the previous decisions or precedents set by courts in similar situations.

Without any equivocation or hesitation, a Black's Law Dictionary is indispensable in interpreting the language of the judges; Black's Law Dictionary not only makes simple the complex principles of jurisprudence, it gives citations, makes translations from Latin, and has an overall mission of making the complex simple. If you see a citation, say 2 F2d 654, it merely means you should see page 654 of the second volume of the series of reported cases known as the second Federal Reporter series. Federal cases are reported to the Federal Reporter System, the Federal Supplement and the Federal Rules Decisions, which are essentially a series of decisions affecting procedural matters.

There is a Federal Digest system, which leads to cases listed in various topics according to alphabetical order. The United States Reports, of course, give us the decisions of the U.S. Supreme Court in Washington, DC and the exact same cases are reported in the series known as Supreme Court Reports and the Lawyers Edition of the Supreme Court Decisions.

Federal Statutes are contained in a volume known as the U.S. Code series. You can find the Federal Rules of Civil Procedure in this series. Check the index. Each of the 50 states has a Digest system, a statute series and a decisions series.

A series known as Sheperds Citation will help you find case decisions matching the citations of a case. Volume numbers and page numbers in the Sheperds Citations will assist you in locating subsequent decisions about the principles raised in the case you are "Sheperdizing."

You should Sheperdize to see if a case has ever been reversed, analyzed or discussed in other litigation.

Any law library worth its salt will have a card catalogue system in alphabetical order based on both subject and author. You can find books and treatises to elaborate on any topic you need, and then there are the Law Reviews. Law Reviews include scholarly essays on relatively narrow issues. Annotated statute books will often lead to Law Review articles and inevitably Law Review articles will lead to more cases, as well as general background, such as legislative intent, that might help win an argument in court.

Legal encyclopedias, such as the American Jurisprudence series, the Corpus Juris series and the ALR are available to give you intense background on the topics you want, in well organized essays categorized and subcategorized on the aspects of the subject you are looking for. For example, an article on property will be divided between real property (real estate) and personal property (chattels).

Every conceivable topic will be discussed such as liens, titles, easements, condominiums, the statute of uses and so forth.

These legal encyclopedias can help bridge the gap between lawyers and laypersons.

When you have a legal problem, you must be able to recognize the concepts that apply to your case. A series like ALR or Corpus Juris can explain the law very succinctly, and will also distinguish what the differences are in the law in certain states where decisions have been reached on it.

Again alphabetical order will help you get through this work, no special mystery exists.

West Publishing Company of St. Paul Minnesota, will be very obvious, publishes perhaps 60% of everything you see in the law library. The volumes you see which are called "Restatements of the Law" are extremely helpful if you want to obtain an in-depth familiarity with a certain subject. The restatement of the law comes from generally recognized principles based on prevailing court decisions in the 50 states.

These books are simple, easy to understand and strongly recommended in order to become familiar relatively rapidly with a specific area.

West has a database service known as Westlaw, which is quite expensive, but can also find legal information very rapidly in any state or in the federal system, sheperdize it for you and printout case after case without you having to photocopy it. Law students get to use it all the time; lawyers outside of the major firms generally do not use Westlaw because it is so expensive - Westlaw's only rival is Lexis, also expensive. Persons have been known to hire law students to access the computer databases for them, and save hundreds of dollars in so doing.

The Code of Federal Regulation lists literally thousands of federal rules and regulations on matters such as copyrights, commodities futures, securities, immigration and naturalization and virtually anything else the federal government claims jurisdiction over. This is available at any government bookstore as well as the law library. Volumes will be sold individually if you wish.

Remember that every statute series has a pocket part section at the end of the volume. Laws get out of date and the pocket parts are simply updates. Many other law books have pocket parts as well.

Many people do not realize their state has a constitution separate from the federal constitution and that every foreign country except one or two has a constitution as well. For a foreign constitution look for a volume "Constitutions of the World." State statute series includes the state constitution.

The General Digest system is an index system to state reporter systems (of cases) updated every ten years. It is an excellent way to look for cases about key topics, all listed in alphabetical order.

Reporter systems exists on a regional basis as well as state by state. For example, a case in Massachusetts may be found in a Mass. Reporter System or the Northeast Reporter System (NE 2d, i.e.) There is a Pacific System, an Atlantic system, an Northwest System, a Southern System, South Eastern Reporter, and Southwestern Reporter. California has an extensive reporting system for itself.

Form books are a popular item in every law library. Series such as the American Jurisprudence Forms Series, Rabkin & Johnson Series, Moore's Federal Practice Series has a Forms series. Forms are needed for both the practice of litigation and for commercial transactions. They are a major part of any lawyer's life. Obviously, quite a bit of very overpriced software now exists for easily accessing forms on disk. Most of the prices are obscene. Use the library photocopier.

Remember that for complex legal transactions you may need the advice or aid of a lawyer to stay out of difficulty.

Digests and indexes exist for legal journals, such as law reviews, bar journals and other scholarly legal periodicals. The law librarian may be of assistance in identifying which indexes are available. It is likely the indexes at the library you are using will be located right next to the card catalogue.

From time to time you may wish to learn the intent of your federal law makers in drafting legislation. Be aware that a volume known as the History of Bills Table exists for each Congressional session which can refer you to the appropriate debate transcript in the Congressional Record. There is a US Code Congressional and Administrative News Service which publishes House and Senate reports on legislation, and whose publications will be found in the reference section.

Books are available on legal research. This author uses Fundamentals of Legal Research by Jacobstein and Mersky, published by Foundation Press in Mineola, New York. However, all of the research technique in the world is useless unless you acquire the basic building blocks of legal knowledge by reading texts such as restatements, some Constitutional case law, make frequent reference to Black's Law Dictionary and learn your Federal Rules of Civil Procedure.

A copy of the latter is available at any federal bookstore for $4.00. The federal bookstore is actually a treasure trove for information. If you live near a major city, visit the nearest one. Not only will you find numerous law books for federal court practice, you will find publications by the Justice Department used to train its personnel.

The Freedom of Information Act (FOIA) and the state versions of this law also help obtain access to Government records. For example, this author once successfully used the FOIA to obtain the training manual of a certain law enforcement agency. An in-depth look at the litigation involving FOIA will give you an understanding of how that law has been used to gain evidence to win cases.

The digest volumes, i.e. General Digests, individual state digest volumes and federal digests all have index volumes in alphabetical order where you can look up key words.

Chapter 3

Introduction to Civil Procedure

Civil Procedure refers to the rules used in court to process the flow of pleadings and motions in civil (non-criminal, non administrative cases) in state and federal courts in the United States. This essay is a brief outline of the Federal Rules of Civil Procedure.

Many states have procedural rules closely mirroring the Federal Rules. According to *Rule 1,* the rules "shall be construed to secure the just, speedy, and inexpensive determination of every action."

Rule 2 states there shall be one form of action to be known as a "civil action" to be commenced, according to *Rule 3,* by filing a complaint in the Court's Clerk's Office; and served with a summons upon the other side according to local rules by either certified mail, constable or other means described by law. (See *Rule 4*)

The methodology of writing a *COMPLAINT* is one of the most critical aspects of law practice.

A complaint must accomplish several things.

1. A complaint must clearly identify the parties.

2. A complaint must describe the reasons you are bringing a lawsuit. The legal and factual reasons should be stated.

3. A complaint must be labeled a complaint, and include numbered paragraphs.

4. The caption on the complaint should include the name of the court. and, in state court, the county.

5. The complaint should explain the jurisdictional basis, i.e. what laws give the court authority to act.

6. The complaint should demand one or more of three kinds of relief.

A. MONEY DAMAGES, including costs, interest and in some cases legal fees where allowed by either contract or law.

B. EQUITABLE RELIEF, divided into

(a) *injunctive relief* - when the court can order a specific action (or prevent one).
or

(b) *declaratory relief* - stating the rights and obligations of parties, the legality of a statute or ownership of title, for example.

If you have been served with a complaint and you want to contest the matter, within the time period called for by law, you must file either an *ANSWER* or a *MOTION TO DISMISS*.

Answers are filed in court and served by mail also on the other side. The answer in court must include a *CERTIFICATE OF SERVICE* which certifies that you sent a copy to all interested parties. All court pleadings require such a certificate.

When you file an answer, you should prepare in a format where the caption is similar to the complaint except you label it *ANSWER*.

You must state that you deny the allegations that are false, paragraph by paragraph, admit those that are accurate.

If you are hesitant to specifically deny or admit, you can give a mealy mouthed answer. This can be "Defendant neither admits nor denies the allegation of Paragraph (#) but calls upon the Plaintiff to prove same." Or "Admitted in part and Denied in part." You may or may not wish to elaborate in your reply.

Both Answers and Pleadings should be signed by the party and include an address and phone number. State whether or not you are *PRO-SE*, (acting without a lawyer.)

If you have a good reason, you can file a Motion to Dismiss instead of an Answer.

Rule 12(b) allows you to file a motion to dismiss for six grounds, in lieu of an answer.

1. **Motion To Dismiss For Lack Of Jurisdiction.** The court has no authority to hear your case due to the subject matter, i.e. workman's compensation cases cannot be filed in municipal courts in Massachusetts or certain statutes of limitations have expired, and jurisdiction expires with them.

2. **Motion To Dismiss For Lack Of Jurisdiction Over The Person.** i.e., If somebody lives in Montana and you want to sue him in Florida, you'd better do some research to justify your suit. The defendant must have sufficient contacts with the state you sue him in to justify a claim of jurisdiction. Sometimes "long arm statutes" permit lawsuits when the defendant has transacted business or caused an injury in a state other than his residence.

3. **Improper Venue**. Suing in the wrong court.

4. **Insufficiency Of Process**. Your constable didn't do the job right or the summons was filled out wrong.

5. **Insufficiency Of Service**. Again, check constable's return.

6. **Failure To State Claim**. Failure to write a proper complaint with a legally recognized grievance.

7. **Failure To Join A Necessary Party**. (See *Rule 19*)

There are a number of other motions available to get rid of a case. In Massachusetts you can file a **Motion To Dismiss For Failure To Properly Name A Defendant**. (i.e. spelling a defendant's name wrong)

If you are a defendant, you can file counterclaims against the plaintiff, cross claims against other defendants, third party complaints against persons partially responsible for the obligation to the plaintiff, if any and a host of other maneuvers to be discussed later.

At some point in time whether you are a plaintiff or defendant you will be interested in gathering evidence from the other side, and from witnesses. This is called *DISCOVERY*.

Discovery, like motion practice, can play a decisive role in the combat between parties.

For example, *Rule 33* allows thirty (30) questions in writing to be propounded to the other side. These questions are known as *Interrogatories*.

Interrogatories are designed to elicit admissions, or leads to admissible, helpful evidence to make your case stronger using the words of the opposition. Generally you can ask 30 questions and obtain a reply in 45 days. If no answers are given, you can begin a default proceeding.

You can also request the documents and tangible objects in the possession of the opposing party by filing a *Request for Production of Documents and Things Pursuant To Rule 34.*

Any documents relevant to the case which are likely to be admissible as evidence in Court or lead to the discovery of admissible evidence.

Canceled checks, deeds, invoices, insurance policies, correspondence, cash register receipts, diaries, credit card records, brokerage records and so forth are examples of records frequently requested and "discoverable."

The essential purpose of discovery is to obtain the evidence or "clues" to successfully defend or prosecute a claim.

The definition of a "document" is quite broad. For example, it may include microfiche, computer disk, video tape and audio tape, but these should be specified in the request to be certain.

As a litigant, you also have the right to inspect premises, examine tangible objects and depose witnesses governed by Federal Rule 30. Any party or witness may be deposed, and the usual procedure is to subpoena non-party witnesses to appear in an attorney's office to give testimony before a court stenographer.

All counsel involved and pro-se parties may cross examine the witness.

The rules have evolved to permit video taped depositions, telephone depositions, and depositions to non-parties by written questions.

Persons living out-of-state or in foreign countries may be deposed according to procedures set by court.

Rule 28(b) permits use of foreign notaries to assume the powers of a stenographer and is also as an enabling authority to allow U.S. diplomatic personnel to administer oaths.

Depositions can be used to contradict statements made by witnesses in court, as can interrogatory replies.

Depositions are mainly used to acquire evidence by asking witnesses what their knowledge is about the circumstances of a case. They can have an intimidating effect. Answers are under oath and subject to perjury laws.

At the conclusion of discovery it is not uncommon for either party to seek to file a *Motion For Summary Judgment*. This is a pleading which asks the court to decide a case prior to trial.

Rule 56 governs motions for summary judgment. In order to obtain summary judgment, you must convince the court through affidavits, exhibits and a brief that no material dispute of facts exists.

That is, in fact, a request to apply the law to facts that are so obvious or agreed to that trial would be superfluous.

Trial is usually the aim of the plaintiff but a result a defendant would prefer to avoid. Occasionally plaintiffs, especially on debt collection cases, bring motions for summary judgment.

Many cases which could conceivably result in monetary awards for the plaintiff before a jury get knocked out in “dispositive” motions such as a Motion For Summary Judgment.

Motion Practice

A *motion* is simply a written or oral request for the Court to do something.

Ideally, a motion is filed on a type written piece of paper under the case caption and name of the court.

The motion should include affidavits, legal briefs, and exhibits to the extent needed to get your point across. Frankly, the longer and more detailed the briefs and affidavits and better typed the better the chances of prevailing.

Well prepared motions frequently can intimidate the other side. Discovery disputes are a frequent source of motions. Rule 11 allows you to recover a fine for defending frivolous motions.

The opposing party may frequently stall or play games in discovery and seek to prevent evidence from getting into your hands.

Rule 37 allows for *Motions To Compel Discovery.* Failure to comply with orders to produce discovery can result in many sanctions, such as default, dismissals or fines.

Ample precedents exist to permit discovery in almost every circumstance. The Federal Rules Decision, Federal Digest and the procedural rules themselves contain ample ammunition for arguments either way in discovery.

Rule 26(b) sets forth the grounds for discovery, and the reasons for *Protective Orders*, i.e. a Motion For A Protective Order to prevent abusive discovery is set forth in *Rule 26(c).*

Rules exist to bring in parties to intervene as a party *(Rule 24)* to bring class actions *(Rules 23, 23.1)* and to substitute parties *(Rule 25).*

This is only a broad overview of the most frequently used Federal Rules.

Specific reference to the rules and to sample pleadings and legal precedents is vital to a full and complete understanding of the law of civil procedure.

Summary Judgment Motions

Very often a pro-se litigant suing a government entity or government officials is faced with a Motion For Summary Judgment.

Under Rule 56 of the Federal Rules of Civil Procedure either party may file motions for summary judgment when there is no material dispute of facts and the moving party is entitled to judgment as a matter of law.

As a practical matter, the summary judgment motion will keep your case from going to a jury of your peers and allow a government or other defendant to avoid the risk of a trial.

Plaintiffs who are bringing debt collection cases also use summary judgment motions together with affidavits as a means of avoiding the expense and logistical problems of a trial.

If you are faced with a summary judgment motion, read it very carefully. The wisest strategy is to look for the arguments being made by your opponent as a means of making your opposition argument.

Repeatedly, this writer has filed motions to amend a complaint when faced with technical hair splitting arguments by government lawyers who have raised immunities and defenses for "public servants." For example, instead of suing "John Doe in his official capacity as Clerk of Courts," just sue John Doe. Instead of suing the "Town of Dana," substitute a defendant by way of motion. They'll come up with a reason why their client should not be sued. If they have an argument that is well briefed and you cannot overcome it, consider rewriting your complaint to circumvent their argument. If a statute of limitation argument is being raised, find other grounds to sue them on instead of the one you are seeking. If civil rights has expired, what about Racketeering? Check the index under "Limitation of Actions."

If they claim that there is no material dispute of fact, think very carefully. Maybe there is. If you have one, submit an affidavit signed by the best witnesses to the events (if it is you, you sign it) and include it with your opposition.

If you are unable to overcome a factual argument because you don't have enough information, file a motion to continue the time period to respond until such time as you have exhausted discovery that is sought evidence from your opponents.

In contract actions, I learned that whenever you plead novation in Massachusetts (that is that a new contract was formed to replace a previous one and terms and conditions no longer applied as originally agreed to) this is always a question for the trier of fact (i.e. jury or judge at a bench trial.) This saved defendants from summary judgment on at least two occasions.

One area of law which is very well developed in summary judgment precedents is that of defamation, i.e. libel and slander. In a libel or slander suit, summary judgment motions are virtually inevitable because there is often a chance that a judge will decide that a statement is constitutionally protected. Then the burden is to show some kind of willful, malicious or reckless conduct to overcome the First Amendment shield.

Depositions, interrogatories, and exhibits of evidence as well as answers to requests for admissions are often used to accompany briefs in support of motion for summary judgment.

Thus one must be very careful in how one responds to questions in depositions and interrogatories... they may come back to haunt you.

Of course, you can use your opponents discovery responses as replies to their motion as appendices to your brief, as well as what ever other evidence you can gather.

Rules and statutes permitting summary judgment normally provide that in circumstances in which summary judgment cannot be granted on the entire case. It might be granted on some of the counts in a complaint. For example, in a complaint that includes counts in negligence, civil rights violations, racketeering and anti-trust violations, a judge might just throw out a negligence count and let the others stand. Why? To sustain any kind of court case, you need to show that you have the elements to make an action. For example, in negligence cases, if you are suing a municipality, and were required to file a letter of notice, i.e. **a presentment letter** and did not, the presentment letter is an essential "ingredient" of the lawsuit. Sometimes slack will be granted, i.e. if you sent in error the presentment letter to the mayor instead of the municipal clerk. Presentment rules are often changed every couple of years for no apparent reason other than to trip up lawyers, many of whom are sued for not sending out presentment letters for their clients correctly.

Elements exist in every cause of action. For example, if you allege anti-trust violations, you have to show in some statutory claims **"a combination in restraint of trade"** and under most statutes an **"impact on interstate commerce."** If your complaint does not spell out these causes of action and you don't have the elements of a cause of action your complaint does not stand a good chance of prevailing in a summary judgment motion. A contract without consideration, or with an underage party, is another example.

Chapter 4

Preparing the Complaint

The most important document any lawsuit has is the complaint. The complaint actually plays a major role in the determination of the results of the case. You can have the strongest case imaginable, but if the complaint is written with a defect you can severely damage your case. Refer to the Appendix for several sample complaints, including that of Paula Corbin Jones v. Clinton. (Appendix A)

The complaint must do a number of things: First, it must identify the court and political entity it is being filed in. For example, federal lawsuits in their complaints must identify the fact that they are being brought in **"The United States District Court."** The accompanying case is being brought in the **Eastern District of Arkansas, Western Division**. Note that the parties are identified, and the complaint states *where* they are defendant and plaintiff. The case is also identified as a *civil action*. The fact that a *jury trial* is requested on the caption should also be noted.

The jurisdiction of the Court by statute to hear the case is spelled out in the opening paragraph, right after a very brief introductory statement, (refer to first page, Jones v. Clinton.) Note that diversity of citizenship alone was sufficient grounds for federal jurisdiction because the amount in controversy was over $50,000.)

Venue is supported in a specific statement and the statutory reference is stated in Paragraph Number 2.

The parties are identified in Paragraphs Numbers 3, 4, and 5.

The facts are spelled out carefully and in precise detail. Each cause of action is separated and described so that all elements of the claim are referred to in each count. Reading the accompanying complaint will help the reader learn the basics of drafting a complaint.

Read Rule 8 of the Federal Rules of Civil Procedure. This carefully explains in simple terms what is required to make a complaint stand up in court. Basically you must identify the jurisdiction or enabling authority for your cause of action (sometimes it is a common law count), a statement of the claim, describing the events, and a demand for judgment. This can be both for money or equitable relief in courts with equity jurisdiction such as a restraining order, injunction or declaratory relief. Federal courts have equity jurisdiction, which also includes the right to order specific performance of an act. Failure to honor an order of the court is generally considered a contempt if it is willful.

Federal courts have what is called pendant jurisdiction of state common law claims if there is reason for federal jurisdiction. This can be diversity jurisdiction, a matter involving a federal statute or federal agency, political entity or employee or some other federal question, including a constitutional question.

In the instant case, the complainant, Ms. Jones, has the benefit of federal statutes and diversity jurisdiction (parties in two or more states with $50,000 or more in dispute.)

Note the selection of the statutes which protect the plaintiff's right to equal protection of the law as well as due process. The deprivation of an interest in state employment and the discrimination against the complainant on the basis of her female gender make the case for federal discrimination. Whether the complainant will have problems because other federal statutes or state remedies for redressing these grievances were not utilized remains to be seen.

The author of every complaint must decide how to characterize a cause of action. This means the complaint can be for several different grounds or one or two, and each selection may or may not be correct. Note there was no cause of action for breach of an implied contract. Nor was there a count for negligence... i.e. negligent infliction of emotional distress or for assault or battery. The lawyers have to decide what their best selections were. The failure to make a case for assault, (for putting the victim in fear of imminent danger) was a choice the lawyers had to make. Perhaps the statute of limitations had run out, (your writer is not familiar with Arkansas law, which governs the time limits because the act occurred in that state.)

Interrogatories

Look at Rule 33 of the Federal Rules of Civil Procedure (FRCP). Notice that you are allowed to serve interrogatories upon the opposing party in your lawsuit.

This is a form of discovery, allowed for the purpose of obtaining information to be used at trial or in a motion to dispose of the case one way or another.

Interrogatories are written questions you pose to prove elements of a claim or defense. The questions you ask must be relevant to the case and calculated to lead to admissible evidence at trial. (See Rule 26 of the FRCP)

In a civil rights case, you want to show any number of things: For example, that the policy or custom or regulation that the defendant acted through was unconstitutional.

So ask the other side through an interrogatory such as:

* Identify each and every communication within your scope of possession or control which makes reference to the possible unconstitutionality of the regulations of the Federal Communications Commission.

(This is a way of trying to get them to do some of the research you need for your case)

* Identify each and every claim made against the Federal Communications Commission from 1990 through January 30, 1995 for violations of constitutional rights of broadcasters.

* Identify and describe each of the claims mentioned in your response to the previous interrogatory was resolved.

* Identify the names and addresses of each complainant.

(Expect all kinds of resistance to an answer. You may have to do a <u>Motion To Compel</u>. Look at the local rules of your federal district court.)

Many of our readers have been victimized by police misuse of confidential informants.

Use interrogatories to learn the identity of confidential informants. Sample:

* Identify the names and addresses of each confidential informant defendants relied upon in making an arrest of plaintiff.

* Identify the names and addresses of each informant the defendants relied upon in determining that the plaintiff was abusing his minor child.

If the defendants balk at responding, follow the instructions in your districts, local rules in trying to resolve a discovery dispute first by discussion with the opposing side. Then bring a **Motion To Compel Answers To Interrogatories** against the other side if they still balk.

Interrogatories can also be used for the following purposes:

1. To discover the identities of witnesses and their addresses and phone numbers.

2. To obtain the other side's version of the facts of an incident.

3. To discover the identity of experts and their opinions.

4. To learn the extent of damages claimed by a party.

5. To identify certain conversations, correspondence or events.

6. To locate internal inconsistencies in the opposing party's position by contradicting what witnesses say or what parties say on the other occasions.

It is likely that the cases you examine will include discovery pleadings as well.

<u>Discovery</u>

Discovery, as stated above, is the process whereby opposing parties in litigation can learn information about each other's case by exchanging documents, answering written questions posed to each other, admitting or denying suggested facts, conducting oral depositions of witnesses in the presence of stenographers and even inspecting land, buildings or objects in each others possession or arranging for medical exams.

In the federal courts, the Federal Rules of Civil Procedure govern discovery. These rules are available from any Federal Government Book Store.

Additionally, the local rules of each federal court include rules on discovery. The clerks office will give a litigant a copy of the local rules.

Major conflicts, often long and protracted occur over disputes about production of documents, interrogatory answers and the scheduling of depositions. But even more basic are disputes over what is discoverable.

According to Rule 26, discovery must be calculated to lead to relevant evidence. This does not necessarily mean that each document requested is going to be admissible just that it would lead to relevant information. As a practical matter, the scope of discovery includes insurance policies, assets which may exist to satisfy a judgment, and even personal diaries.

A common problem faced by pro-se litigants is the lack of a format for serving discovery on the opposition. It is not a bad idea to serve interrogatories and requests for production of documents together with the complaint. This does several things: (1) it makes it more expensive for the opponent to defend. (2) it makes it more overwhelming for the opponent to deal with. (3) it makes certain that you will have time to do follow-up discovery on the initial response. (4) it will take time pressure off of you in the future, and allow you to request that all discovery be answered before any hearing on a motion to dismiss.

Examples of discovery pleadings are available in the law libraries. The American Jurisprudence Forms volumes will give you ideas, as will inspecting the litigation files of active suits in the clerk's office. Remember, these are public records. Discovery is what often makes lawsuits long, expensive and vicious. Rule 26(c) includes the opportunity for a party to seek what is called a "protective order" if discovery becomes too burdensome. Rule 27 allows for a deposition to be brought in any situation where even if suit has not been filed, there is a need to perpetuate testimony.

Rules 28 through 32 all govern depositions. You can call a deposition in your home by serving notice and hiring an official stenographer. It is important to remember that a deposition may be introduced into open court to contradict testimony and that answering a deposition is for all purposes similar to testifying in court.

Rule 33 governs interrogatories; these are written questions each can send to the other parties which must be answered within 30 days. Rule 34 governs document requests. Rule 35 allows you or the other side to request a medical or even psychiatric exam of the opposing party.

Rule 36 permits parties to serve requests for admissions upon each other. Litigants merely prepare a list of statements that you want admitted or denied.

Example: (1) that the defendant is in possession of a 1990 Dodge Ram pick up truck. (2) that one Mary Moe was struck with a 1990 Dodge Ram pick up truck which belongs to the defendant. (3) that the defendant resides at 21 Main Street, Gazemont, Iowa.

Rule 37 governs what to do in the event of a discovery dispute. Judges prefer that parties work out discovery disputes among themselves. But often judicial intervention is needed, and this can unbelievably complicate and delay litigation and make the bills mount if you have a lawyer.

Thanks to tough enforcement of Federal Rule 37, sanctions, fines, contempt findings and limitations on the introduction of evidence are the inevitable consequences of unreasonable behavior in discovery. Whoever gets involved in a dispute in court should understand that they will soon be living in a fishbowl.The oposing party gets to learn about many aspects of your life and business.

Model the discovery pleadings to suit your specific needs. Remember the purpose of discovery is to:

1. Find evidence you can introduce into trial.
2. Learn things about your opposition to discredit them at trial.
3. Learn the strengths and weaknesses of your case.
4. Learn the strengths and weaknesses of your opponents.
5. Discover your assets your opponent may have to satisfy a judgement.
6. Discover insurance coverage your opponent may have to satisfy a judgement.
7. Learn about the strengths and abilities of your opponent's counsel. Find out if he strenuously and effectively objects to items you ask for in discovery.
8. Cause your opponents to spend time and money in discovery compliance.
9. Annoy and embarrass the opponent by forcing them to reveal things in discovery they would rather not reveal.

10. If you are a defendant, cause significant delay in the case by forcing the enemy to focus on discovery.

In reality, items 8, 9 and 10 are far from the spirit of an ethical legal practice.

But the truth is that is how many lawyers, if not the overwhelming majority who are serious litigation lawyers, use discovery.

And as a pro-se litigant, you can be sure you will be faced with these tactics.

Automatic Disclosures

There are new rules rapidly emerging in some Divorce Courts and some Federal Courts concerning discovery. The rules forbid a party to begin discovery until the party has complied with what are called Automatic Self Disclosure rules. These rules require you to provide certain categories of information to your opponent and vice versa before you start serving things like deposition notices, interrogatories or document requests. In divorce cases these categories usually relate to financial information and records. In federal litigation the courts are more likely to require automatic disclosure of documents, insurance coverages and witness lists.

Only when these rules are complied with can you then begin discovery.

How do you know when these rules apply? Check the local rules, or ask at the clerk's office where you can obtain the local rules if you don't have them.

Serving Process

Once you have a complaint, it is necessary to serve the complaint, together with the summons and any of the documents required by the Court (i.e. tracking order, cover sheets, statement of damages) upon your opponent in the time span and in manner as specified by the rules of the court you are in. Remember that federal courts have local rules as well as the Federal Rules of Civil Procedure.

If you want to overwhelm and wear down your opponent and make sure he will have to pay more to a defense counsel, serve the defendant with discovery pleadings.

Asset Grabbing for Fun and Profit

A major reason why people sue is to recover money. But if you don't know the procedural rules for collecting money judgments, attaching property, reaching and applying through "equitable attachments" or similar techniques, you can lose the case even if you've won it. And this happens to lawyers and their clients over and over again. There are always uncollectible judgments piling up in law offices across the nation, and in fact, the collection law specialists are often called upon to recover judgments when trial lawyers win a judgment in which there is no insurance coverage.

State remedies differ on how property can be seized. Some states, like Massachusetts, permit ex parte and pre-trial attachments. This means you can start freezing your opponent's property and bank accounts before you win the case and in many cases even without giving him notice.

"Ex parte" means without a party being present. Court rules in Massachusetts permit attachments of property and bank accounts without notice to the alleged debtor provided that a showing can be made of a likelihood of success on the merits, and that a showing can be made that the assets may be conveyed if notice is given, and that no insurance coverage is known to be available to satisfy a judgment.

Naturally, a written motion is required together with an affidavit. Such forms are available in books of legal forms found in law libraries. One can also look through pleadings on file in cases at the local clerk's offices.

A form known as a Writ of Attachment is also required, and is sold by the Court. Once the writ is signed it is served by the sheriff and then either recorded at the Registry of Deeds where it clouds real estate title or, in the event you want to seize the cash receipts of a business, one can use the writ of attachment to install a keeper, that is a person selected by the sheriffs to take all money coming into a cash register in a restaurant, grocery shop or other business.

Sometimes you want to seize cash or other valuables in the hands of third parties. Wages, commissions, insurance settlements, stock certificates, bank accounts and dividend checks are examples of what canny lawyers look for when a target defendant has no insurance. In Massachusetts, the procedural rules allow for what is called a Trustee Process Summons to freeze money that is in the hands of a third party. This is a writ that is prepared by the Plaintiff and submitted to the Court with the motion and affidavit. Naturally the debtor gets no notice, because anybody who knows that their bank account is about to be seized is going to make a withdrawal pretty fast!

Sometimes it is necessary to use procedures in equity to freeze or seize assets. In Massachusetts there are what is known as "reach and apply" actions which permit you to freeze assets that are in the hands of third parties once you have a judgment, by means of direct involvement of the Court.

However, Massachusetts law will also permit pre-trial, exparte injunctions against custodians of stock certificates, companies owing commissions, publishing houses owing royalties and other third parties that may be paying a stream of monies to a debtor from paying any monies to the debtor until further order of the Court.

The injunction will be granted provided a showing can be made that there is a likelihood of prevailing in the case, that irreparable harm would result otherwise and that the comparable damages to the moving party would be greater that to the opposing party.

Under the Federal Rules of Civil Procedure, the state remedies for attachments and other measures to freeze assets are used in the United States District Courts; therefore you must learn state procedure no matter what court you are litigating in, and obtain the correct model forms.

Model Your Pleadings

Let's suppose your neighbor is dumping garbage on your lawn and it is causing you emotional distress. You look in a "key word" index ina law digest or statute book.

"Neighbors," "garbage," and "emotional distress" all come to mind. So do "trespass," "nuisance," and "harassment."

Look up these words and find cases that have a similar subject matter.

When you find them, refer to the introductory captions that contain the name of the court and the docket number.

It is possible to visit or call the court clerk's office and order a complete set of all the pleadings that were filed in the case. Naturally, you will prefer to locate a case from a court nearby, but it is not difficult to contact a court 3,000 miles away and order the documents.

If your lawsuit is based in federal law, it is best to get a precedent from the same circuit that your case will be in, though federal courts often respect what their colleagues across the nation are doing. If you have a state cause of action, it is clearly important to concentrate your research to your state, though if an out of state court had adopted a principle of law that your own state has yet to do, then by all means focus in on it and be sure you have a copy of the decision or statute that might be persuasive.

The file you locate from the clerk's office will unquestionably contain a complaint. When you have the complaint in hand you can examine it to determine how it is similar to your case and how you can rewrite to reflect you grievance. The names of the parties will differ, and you will substitute those. Factual allegations, dates, times, locations will be altered, but the general principles of law, how the elements of the legal cause of action are pled, and how the complaint is structured should be carefully cloned to your fresh complaint.

This is exactly what goes on in law offices across America every single day of the week!

You will also find an answer in the file or a document known as a dispositive motion.

You see, when the sheriffs serve your opponent with the complaint, most courts will give them about 20 days to file what is called a "responsive pleading." This takes the form of an answer which will admit or deny the allegations of the complaint.

Some defendants will not file an answer. They will file a motion to dismiss or for "summary judgment" and argue that the claim is so apparently defective that it should not go forward and be thrown out of court immediately.

Other alternatives open to a defendant include filing a counterclaim with an answer or joining other defendants for indemnification or contribution. This means that the defendant basically says that "if I did anything wrong, so did Mr. Jones, so let's sue him too."

Chapter 5

An Outline of Some Concepts in Civil Law

The most basic way of analyzing a legal situation for a possible cause of action is to determine if the elements of a claim are present. This essay will deal with some of the concepts you'll need to understand when bringing a lawsuit for money damages, or a *civil* suit, as opposed to being involved in a *criminal* matter, in court.

Lawsuits are brought for many reasons, but before you can start a lawsuit, you are best advised to know some of the various different causes of action you can sue for and what you need to prove them.

It is worth having some familiarity with the law of contracts in the course of your legal studies.

More cases are brought for breach of contract, including non-payment for contracts, than for any other cause of action. Remember the elements of a *contract.* You need to keep in mind the following:

1. There must be a lawful purpose to the agreement for it to be enforceable.

2. There must be an offer and acceptance, or actions be parties from which one may infer offer and acceptance.

3. There must be something of value exchanged, called consideration, by the parties.

4. Each party must have lawful capacity to enter into a contract. That is, a party cannot be under the age of 18, insane or otherwise mentally disabled, or intoxicated.

5. There must be mutual assent, or a meeting of the minds, for a contract to be enforceable.

Contracts can be written or oral, but there is a risk that a spoken contract can be voided by a court based on the statute of frauds. The statute of frauds generally states that a contract over $500.00, or involving an obligation to be responsible for the debts of a third party, or a contract to be performed in over one year's time, must be in writing. The statute of fraud is not uniformly enforced, but it is good law in Massachusetts and probably most other states.

Contracts need not be completed to be enforced. People can expect to be paid for substantially performing a contract, substantial performance being a legal concept which you should understand as fulfilling the bulk of one's responsibilities under an agreement.

When one party does not follow its obligations under a contract, it is called a **breach.**

The law also recognizes cases brought under **quantum meruit**, which is a form of "quasi contract." The central theme of a case brought under quantum meruit is that even if there is no precise contract, the person making the claim had a reasonable expectation that she would be compensated for her services and the Court, if the case goes to trial, will then determine what the amount ought to be.

Another major variety of cases falls under the category of **injuries**. There are injuries to people, injuries to property, injuries to reputation and there are intentional and unintentional injuries.

A common type of lawsuit for injuries is the claim for the negligent operation of a motor vehicle which produced injuries. Negligence simply means that the defendant breached a duty of reasonable care which he owed to another, and that breach was the proximate cause of the injury.

But there are many kinds of negligence which produce many kinds of injury.

A newspaper can negligently defame somebody, causing an injury to a person's reputation.

A police force can negligently train or supervise a policeman, causing an injury to a person's liberty or, cause that person to be hit with excessive force.

A common cause of action against a landlord includes claims for negligent infliction of emotional distress.

What happens when a company's employee acts negligently? The company can be held responsible under a doctrine known as ***respondeat superior*** for the negligence of employees and servants.

Some injuries are, of course, caused intentionally, even though they are claims made in a court for money damages, instead of criminal actions. They are called "torts" or "civil wrongs" whether intentional or unintentional.

Trespass, the unauthorized entry to another person's land or chattels, i.e. movable property, such as an automobile or horse, is a kind of intentional act.

Assault, which is placing a person in fear of immediate danger, is also a recognized claim in a civil lawsuit.

Battery is an **unpermitted touching** which, again, is a grounds for suing a person civilly.

Tortious Conversion is a grounds for suing a person, or a company, for taking property of another and using it for the defendant's benefit with the intent to deprive the rightful owner of the use, possession and benefit of it. For example, let's say your company has an employee and she steals a chemical formula or a mailing list that belongs to the company and uses it for her own purposes or sells it. The employee can be held liable for tortious conversion.

Libel and slander are examples of intentional torts which cause injury to a person's reputation.

Libel refers to a published communication which holds a person to scorn, contempt or ridicule.

Slander refers to spoken words.

Our readers should also be aware of the concept of **constitutional torts.**

Constitutional torts are claims resulting from persons being deprived of their civil rights. In addition to the many kinds of claims which can be brought against some government employees under the federal civil rights acts, there are also claims based under state law, which do not necessarily involve government action. False arrest claims for example, are often made against police officers, supermarket and department store security personnel and others for wrongfully depriving persons of their liberty.

False imprisonment claims are also made for example, against retail store personnel by persons who are detained under accusation of shoplifting.

Title 42 United States Code Section 1983 is a commonly used federal civil rights statute which makes depriving persons of constitutional rights under "color of law" i.e with state, municipal or county involvement, actionable. However, as a practical matter many of the persons who are most likely to deprive you of your civil rights, such as judges, court appointed guardians, court clerks, child protection service workers and opposing lawyers, are almost always immune from lawsuits under the civil rights acts.

Bivens actions are lawsuits brought directly under the Constitution, often with one of the Bill of Rights as enabling jurisdiction, for a civil rights violation by a federal as opposed to a state employee. Complaints of both varieties are reprinted in Appendix B & C

A very brief overview of the kinds of constitutional rights you may be litigating over is as follows:

1 Your First Amendment rights, which allow you to express opinions, criticize government, demonstrate and picket, and be free from the trappings or semblance of a state sponsored religion.

2. Your Second Amendment rights, which, in my view and the view of many, permit individuals the right to keep arms.

3. Your Fourth Amendment right to be free from unreasonable search and seizure, the right to be free in your home or place of business and to have your personal papers and possessions free from confiscation by government agents, unless they obtain a warrant. This right has been eroded significantly by the subpoena power of administrative agencies.

4. Your rights under the Fifth Amendment, which offers a wide range of protections against abuses of government authority in the administration of judicial proceedings, in the taking of private property for government use (requiring just compensation for such action) and in preventing persons from being forced to incriminate themselves. But much more broadly, the Fifth Amendment and Fourteenth Amendment offer protections for your rights to due process, your right to have notice and a fair and meaningful hearing, and, in theory, to be free from any kind of arbitrary and capricious state action which would shock the conscience. The Fourteenth Amendment offers you protection against abuses at the state level, the Fifth Amendment offers you protection form federal due process violations.

5. The Sixth Amendment, which allows you the right to counsel of your choice, and to be afforded counsel if you cannot afford it in matters where a jail sentence is possible, and the right to confront witnesses against you. Of course, under present law, the right to counsel does not include the right to unlicensed counsel.

6. The Eighth Amendment, which is your protection against excessive bail or excessive fines, and cruel and unusual punishment.

7 The Ninth Amendment, which guarantees you the enjoyment of natural rights not specified in the Constitution. The right to privacy, the right to travel, the right of family autonomy, to parenting, to your choice of medical options; these are some of the Ninth Amendment rights which are still being litigated from time to time.

8. The Fourteenth Amendment, which offers you protection from abuses by state, municipal or county government of your right to due process and to be free from discrimination.

Few lawyers ever bother to learn the distinction between procedural and substantive due process, but you should. When state or local government abuses you so outrageously, and their treatment shocks the conscience, that's when you may have a claim for violation of your substantive due process rights.

But when the course of the system's deciding the outcome of your case is flawed by bias, deprivations of notice or a hearing, inadequate safeguards of fairness, then you may have a claim for deprivation of procedural due process.

Sometimes you may not learn that you have been sued because the process server has not properly served you with the complaint. In such cases you can lose before having your date in court, and that is an example of being denied procedural due process under the Fifth Amendment, and is, of course, grounds for a lawsuit under the 5th and 14th amendments.

Equitable Relief

Sometimes asking the court for just money won't solve your legal problem.

There are times you'll need i*njunctive relie*f, which is a court order to do something or to refrain from doing something. Violations of an injunction are a contempt of court which can be punished by a jail term. You can ask for an injunction by filing motion.

Declaratory relief is another form of remedy the court offers. It is basically relief in the form of a ruling by the judge about the legal status of a sitaution. It can be a ruling as to the ownership of property, whether real estate or personal, or the constitutionality of a statute, or rights under a contract, for a few examples.

A complaint can ask for an injuction or declarartory relief as well as money damages.
There is also a form of relief known as *specific performace,* which is a prayer for relief seeking the conveyance of a unique item, such as a painting or piece of real estate, that is by its nature a one of a kind item. The prayer for sepcific performace is usually a remedy for breach of contract.

Chapter 6

Helen versus Frank's Department Store

Helen was shopping in Frank's Department Store in the quaint Massachusetts resort beach town of South Harbor.

While browsing along the aisles examining blouses, socks and the other garments, she caught the attention of a security guard from Whackenspot Protective Services, a private company under contract to guard the merchandise in Frank's Department Store.

Helen picked up a blouse and a pair of socks and walked past the cash registers toward a snack bar within the department store.

A female guard grabbed her arm and said, "Please come with me ma'am." Helen was shocked. She was frightened and speechless. Her friends and neighbors saw her being escorted, and she saw them. She felt her heart race and butterflies flitter inside her stomach.

Helen was taken to a room near the back of the store and asked to sign a confession that she stole several items from the store. In exchange for her signing the confession, she was told she could leave the store.

Helen finally gained her composure. "I will not sign this document. I demand to talk to my lawyer."

The security guard called the store manager. After a brief discussion, Helen was asked to leave the store.

After the incident was reviewed with the store's attorney, a decision was made not to prosecute Helen. (The arrest was improper because Helen had never left the store with the goods.)

Helen had a friend named Jill who was a law student. Helen hated lawyers. She decided she wanted to teach the Department Store a lesson, on her own, in court.

First, she sent demand letters under Massachusetts' Consumer Protection Act. This law makes all unfair and deceptive practices in business illegal. The statute allows any consumer to send a demand letter to a company to seek redress of grievances within 30 days. The statute requires the company to make a good faith investigation and a reasonable settlement offer, if one is required. If the company does not act in good faith after receiving the letter, the company can be held liable for triple damages and the consumer's legal fees (MGL Ch. 93A §2).

Helen sent a letter to the store manager under the Act, and to Whackenspot.

She complained of false arrest, false imprisonment, intentional infliction of emotional distress and violation of the Consumer Protection Act, as well as the State Civil Rights Act, which makes any violation of Constitutional Rights using "threats, coercion or intimidation" actionable (i.e. you can sue for it).

Frank's Department Store did not respond to Helen's letter, but she sent it certified mail and held onto the receipt. Whackenspot failed to send a reply as well.

Jill helped her write a complaint, which she filed at the local courthouse and which she served on Frank's Department Store, in which she asked for a jury trial. Whackenspot and the security guard were named as codefendants. Helen sued for both common law and statutory causes of action.

In the meantime, Helen had a visit with a psychiatrist, who determined that as a result of the incident, Helen was suffering from a variety of post-traumatic stress disorders, including sleeplessness, depression, and anxiety. She was nervous at work and very hesitant to enter stores.

COMMONWEALTH OF MASSACHUSETTS

CLAM BAY COUNTY

SOUTH HARBOR
SUPERIOR COURT
CIVIL DOCKET NO.

HELEN GAZEMONT
Plaintiff

v.

FRANK'S DEPARTMENT STORE, INC., WHACKENSPOT PROTECTIVE SERVICES CORPORATION and HELGA SWANSEN,
Defendants

COMPLAINT AND JURY DEMAND

Background Summary

This is an action for false arrest, unfair and deceptive business practices, negligence, false imprisonment, violations of the Massachusetts Civil Rights Act (GL Ch. 12 §11I) and intentional infliction of emotional distress.

Parties

1. Helen Gazemont is an individual residing at 74 Maple Lane in South Harbor, Massachusetts. She is the Plaintiff in the above captioned proceeding.

2. Frank's Department Store, Inc. Is a business corporation with a usual place of business at 734 Lincoln Street in South Harbor, Massachusetts.

3. Helga Swansen is an individual residing at 59 Elm Street in Wilton, Massachusetts.

4. Whackenspot Protective Services Corporation is a business corporation with a usual place of business in South Dakota.

Causes of Action

5. Paragraphs one through four are realleged and reinstated herein.

6. On or about January 14, 1998 the Plaintiff was a business invitee at Frank's Department Store in South Harbor when she was subjected to a humiliating and groundless arrest by the defendants.

7. The Plaintiff was physically apprehended by the Defendants, their agents, servants and employees and transported to a small room and badgered about signing a confession to larceny. She declined to sign a confession.

8. The Plaintiff was held in confinement against her will for approximately 27 minutes and humiliated in front of her neighbors and friends.

9. At no time did Defendants have probable cause to arrest the Plaintiff.

10. As a consequence of the false arrest by the Defendants, the Plaintiff suffered tremendous pain of mind and required medical attention.

Count Two
False Imprisonment

11. Each of the allegations stated in paragraphs one through ten above are realleged and restated herein.

12. The defendants wrongfully, falsely and without probable cause or any reasonable justification, imprisoned the Plaintiff.

13. The Plaintiff was damaged thereby.

Count Three
Violation of G.L. Ch. 12 §11I

14. Each of the allegations stated in paragraphs one through ten above are realleged and restated herein.

15. At all times relevant herein, the Plaintiff enjoyed rights as a citizen in her person and to be free from false arrest and false imprisonment, as well as self-incrimination.

16. Using force, threats and coercion, in falsely arresting and wrongfully confining her, and attempting to coerce her into signing a confession, Defendants' and their agent or servant or employee Helga Swansen deprived the Plaintiff of her Civil Rights in violation of G.L. Ch. 12 §11I.

17. Plaintiff was damaged thereby.

Count Four
Unfair Business Practice

18. Each of the allegations stated above in paragraphs one through ten are realleged herein and made a part of this paragraph.

19. The Defendant's Whackenspot and Frank's Department Store each received a copy of the letter affixed herein as Exhibit "A" complaining of the abusive treatment the Plaintiff received from the agent, servant or employee and asked for compensation.

20. Under Mass G.L. Ch. 93A the Defendants were obligated to respond to the letter within thirty (30) days after conducting a full investigation.

21. Defendants were further recognized to make a good faith offer to compromise the claim.

22. The Defendants engaged in an unfair business practice by falsely arresting and imprisoning the Plaintiff, and attempting to coerce a confession from her.

23. The Plaintiff suffered damages thereby .

Count Five
Negligence

24. Each allegation previously stated is reincorporated herein and made a part of this paragraph.

25. The Defendant's owed a duty to properly hire, train, and supervise, securing personnel to respect the Constitutional rights of shoppers.

26. The Defendant's breached said duty.

27. The Plaintiff was damaged thereby.

Count Six
Intentional Infliction of Emotional Distress

28. Each allegation previously stated is reincorporated herein and made a part of this paragraph.

29. The actions of the defendants were so outrageous and reprehensible that they shock the conscious of responsible people in a civilized community and no reasonable person should be required to endure them.

30. Plaintiff was damaged thereby.

Wherefore Plaintiff urges this court to award her such damages as a jury of her peers deems appropriate and just.

Helen Grazemont
Plaintiff Pro-se

____

74 Maple Lane
South Harbor, MA
Phone: 123-987-6543

Now, without a doubt Helen would get the attention of the Department Stores.

They would have a hard time in getting this complaint dismissed, because Helen has pretty much plead the elements of the various Causes of Action.

It is important to note that the Causes of Action in Civil Rights do not include "respondeat superior," i.e. the employer being liable for the actions of a subordinate. The best way to get at the employer in a Civil Rights situation is through common law remedies, including negligent hiring, training and supervision.

Once Helen sues and serves the Defendants, it is time to start thinking about discovery.

Document requests should seek incident reports, video tapes, the personnel files of all employees who witnessed or participated in the incident, past complaints about similar incidents, the contract between the two corporate Defendants, and other specifically named items that might help establish damages.

Helen's psychiatrist is an important witness, as are other shoppers who may have witnessed the event.

Federal Civil Rights actions are inappropriate in this case because government is not involved. However, Massachusetts has a State Civil Rights Act that allows lawsuits against private parties for civil rights violations involving threats, coercion and/or intimidation.

At trial, Helen can win pro-se. She must get on the stand and tell the jury her story calmly and steadily. She should place her witness on the stand, ask the questions, and object to any questions by the Defendants that are irrelevant, immaterial, or more prejudicial than probative. The judge will decide the evidentiary objection.

She should anticipate objections by the defense to her statements.

It is important that she testify to what happened, what she saw, what she experienced.

Opinions and conclusions are excluded except when given by experts such as her psychiatrist.

More Comments on False Arrest Cases

It is generally easier to recover a settlement from a private company for false arrest than from a government entity.

Private companies are usually represented by lawyers retained by insurance companies who are conscious of risks posed by an outraged jury. They also realize that it is expensive to go to trial and that offering a claimant the costs of defense (or less) is a good strategy.

Government entities do not see it that way. They often have the arrogance, indifference to expense and callous disregard for justice that breeds protracted litigation, dirty tactics, and the use of procedural minutia to make the case as painful as possible for you.

Often they will submerge a claimant in reams of paper. Once in a false arrest case, our client was made to answer 294 interrogatories!

The government lawyers who defend civil rights cases often practice in no other area. They read everything published on the subject and are formidable opponents.

Chapter 7

What Entrepreneurs Need to Know about Business Torts

A major problem for entrepreneurs in litigation is that very often courts will insist that a corporation, other than in small claims court, be represented by a lawyer. Many times the way to get around this is to bring an action as a shareholder, as a shareholder derivative suit, stating that the corporation, having been notified (usually by certified mail) that there is cause to bring an action fails to do so, and that the shareholder brings this action in her capacity as a shareholder for herself and others similarly situated.

If you or your business have been the victim of an unscrupulous business practice, you should know about business torts, causes of action pled in court to seek redress for non-criminal, wrongful conduct that has damaged you.

Earlier in this book we discussed contracts and what constitutes a *breach*. Breach of contract is a very common cause of action in business disputes, for obvious reasons. When companies do business with each other, something is always bound to go wrong, either innocently or deliberately. Very often the way a business may breach a contract is to just not pay the bill, or not pay all of the bill.

Sometimes business persons do act maliciously or overreach in their transactions.

What happens when a company induces another company to enter into a business relationship by misrepresenting important information or leaving out important information? Companies, of course, can sue each other for deceit!

In fact, states like Massachusetts and California have made any unfair or deceptive act in business illegal, allowing victims to sue for triple damages. One would label the cause of action "Unfair and deceptive business practices."

Another example of wrongful conduct is what is called "tortious interference with an advantageous relationship." This occurs when a defendant knows that the victim enjoys a good relationship with an individual or group of individuals, that the relationship tends to be beneficial to the victim, and the defendant does something wrongful to interfere with the relationship causing harm.

An example might be to claim that a restaurant owner is a racist so that black people stop coming to his restaurant. Or to intimidate or threaten people on their way into a shop.

Another may be to spread a rumor that ten percent of a company's profits are donated to the Church of Satan.

Similar is the cause of action known as *tortious interference with contractual relations*. This is wrongful interference with a definite contractual relationship, causing a party to breach its contract with the plaintiff.

Tortious conversion is quite close to stealing, in my opinion. Barbara F. works at a high tech company, copies down information about a trade secret, and sells it to her employer's competitor. This is an example of conversion, which is technically defined as depriving the owner of something of the benefit of ownership rights. If the employer decided to sue Barbara F., they would sue her for tortious conversion.

More sophisticated and complex situations sometimes call for the application of more complex laws.

The RICO Act, Title 18 US Code Section 1964, which stands for Racketeer Influenced Corrupt Organizations, has a civil section which enables victims to bring lawsuits against individuals or businesses which engage in serious, usually systematic, criminal or virtually criminal conduct involving such actions as fraud, threats of violence, violence, corrupting government officials, extortion, and similar types of activity, involving interstate commerce or the means of interstate commerce. Very often, victims of investment fraud have sued under RICO. Because it allows for attorneys fees and punitive damages, the statute was popular with lawyers for a while, but grew into disfavor as defendants fought back vigorously, winning sanctions against those who were too loose to label their adversaries as "racketeers," and also convincing the court that very technical aspects of the law had to be successfully pled in order to recover. Clearly, nobody should attempt to sue anybody for racketeering, unless they really know what they are doing, or are prepared to face a fine for frivolous pleading.

Although RICO is a federal cause of action, some states allow it to be pled in state courts, or have a state version of the law.

Common law *conspiracy* is a cause of action in its own right, but must be pled in cojunction with another tort, such as deceit, conversion or other wrongful conduct. Technically, pleading conspiracy requires the plaintiff to allege the defendant engaged in a number of acts, some lawful, perhaps some not, for an unlawful purpose, in concert with others. All of the conspirators should be sued, or named as John Doe I, John Doe II, Jane Doe I, etc. if their identities are unknown.

Very often, wrongful business activities can be plead as conspiracies, because they will involve two or more persons acting in concert and may run afoul of the law.

Chapter 8

Making a Federal Case Out Of It

When is a legal case properly brought in federal court?

Federal courts, such as the United States District Court in Boston, have the power to hear certain kinds of cases falling into two main categories:

1. When a controversy involves an amount in question greater than $50,000 and a diversity of citizenship, i.e. when the parties to the lawsuit live in two or more states.

2. When a federal question is involved. This could mean a lawsuit brought under a federal statute. Civil rights lawsuits, securities fraud lawsuits, social security matters, anti-trust lawsuits, copyrights and patents - these all involve a federal statute and federal courts have jurisdiction or power to hear them.

   Additionally, whenever a federal agency or the United States of America itself is a party to a claim, the federal courts have jurisdiction.

The right to a jury trial in federal court is guaranteed under the Seventh Amendment of the U.S. Constitution, in most circumstances. This amendment states:

> In suits at common law, where the value in controversy shall exceed $20.00 the right of a jury trial shall be preserved, and no fact tried by a jury shall otherwise be re-examined in any Court of the United States, than according to the rules of the common law.

In addition, the federal courts have what are known as "equitable powers". This means they have the power to order kinds of relief other than money damages.
Equity relief includes:

1. Restraining orders, such as preventing a company from doing business, or from engaging in a certain practice (such as dumping hazardous chemicals near a certain location) or orders which prevent someone from engaging in a certain conduct.

2. Injunctions. These are court orders instructing a party to perform a certain act. Court ordered desegregation, the break up in the telephone company and similar kinds of extraordinary relief are examples of injunctions.

3. Declaratory relief. Federal courts have the power to make a legally binding interpretation of law or fact, especially a dispute of a contractual nature or statutory interpretation, which can be binding on parties. They can determine ownership of a property, rights under an insurance policy or the constitutionality of a state or federal law or regulation or even a municipal ordinance.

Federal courts have the right and authority to order changes in state, local and county governments.

Federal courts can monitor developments in prison systems, police departments and other governmental bodies to ensure that no constitutional guarantees are being violated, i.e. use of excessive force, harassment, etc.

Any individual can institute a civil complaint in federal court to ask for protection from a state or local government body under the federal civil rights laws (Title 42, Section 1983) when such a constitutional wrong has occurred and ask for injunctive relief, a restraining order and money damages.

Although the federal courts do have power to dismiss complaints if they do not conform to federal rules, the general policy is to be lenient when civil rights complainants try to represent themselves and draft their own complaints.

The cost of filing a complaint in federal court is $150.00; if one is financially in difficult straits, the fee may be waived.

Chapter 9

Federal Civil Rights Statutes

Time does not permit me to know each of you personally, but I feel a special responsibility to each and every one of you for helping launch what for me is a difficult and challenging, though spiritually fulfilling project.

If there is one statute I think is the most important one for all Americans to know, it would be Title 42 U.S. Code § 1983, which reads as follows:

> Every person who, under color of any statute, ordinance, regulation, custom, or usage of any State of Territory subjects or causes to be subjected, any citizen of the United States or other person within the jurisdiction thereof to the deprivation of any rights, privilege, or immunities secured by the Constitution and laws, shall be liable to the party injured in an action at law, suit in equity, or other proper proceeding for redress.

This essentially makes unconstitutional conduct illegal and actionable. This statute is a weapon for citizens to use against state, local, and county government (it rarely applies to federal employees; that is another subject altogether) and allows cases to be brought into federal court without exhaustion of remedies at the state level.

Capricious zoning boards, extorting building inspectors, bullying cops, racist bureaucrats and anybody else who denies you of equal protection and due process is subject to these laws, so long as there is some state involvement or county or municipal involvement in their actions.

What if a government official entrusted with protecting your rights fails to act?

Title 42 § 1986 states that:

> Every person having knowledge that any of the wrongs... are about to be committed and having the power to prevent or aid in preventing the commission of the same, neglects or refuses so to do... shall be liable...

As was stated in our essay "How To Sue a Judge" judges are not entirely immune from lawsuits under the federal civil rights laws. They may be sued for declaratory and injunctive relief, unless they act outside of their jurisdiction. If they act outside of their jurisdiction, they may be sued for money damages as well. Under the Federal Courts Improvement Act of 1996, the ability to sue a judge has been greatly curtailed.

Poor prison conditions may violate the Eighth Amendment right to be free from cruel and unusual punishment.

Warrantless invasions of a home by police may violate the Fourth Amendment right to be free from unreasonable searches and seizures.

Malicious prosecutions by police may violate the right to due process of the law under the Fifth and Fourteenth Amendments.

False arrests and false imprisonment may violate the right to be free from unreasonable searches and seizures under the Fourth Amendment.

Expelling a student from a state school or firing a teacher at a state school or college for expressing a point of view may violate the First Amendment.

For a very broad description of some other rights or causes of action not commonly understood and falling into both natural rights and historical personal rights at common law, one should carefully study the Ninth Amendment.

The Ninth Amendment reads as follows:

> The enumeration in the Constitution of certain rights shall not be construed to deny or disparage others retained by the people.

Few lawyers are familiar with this, but, in fact, the Ninth Amendment is so broad as to open up areas of constitutional litigation that have probably been missed in the past. Natural rights, the right to own, acquire, or alienate property, certain privacy rights, right to a livelihood, and host of others which are of great importance in overcoming obstacles to characterizing a cause of action.

There is only one or two cases involving the Ninth Amendment in the history of the Supreme Court which discuss the law in depth. In *Griswald v. Connecticut* the right to marital privacy was upheld as a Ninth Amendment right. The case involved contraception.

Cases involving state and municipal licensing boards and cases involving the overregulation of any human or commercial endeavor should be analyzed with a view to using the Ninth Amendment as a possible means of redress, as well as other constitutional amendments.

Litigating a federal civil rights case is not easy. While the law reads nicely on paper, courts have evolved an intricate web of defenses and excuses for not awarding damages to the victims of some of the worst kinds of unconstitutional conduct. Doctrines such as qualified immunity and absolute immunity have evolved to shield some of the worst offenders.

For example, it is extremely difficult to sue child protective care workers, except in some limited circumstances. And the abstention doctrine *(Younger v. Harris)* will be used to prevent a federal lawsuit seeking to block a state prosecution by means of injunction. Prosecutors can be sued if they do things out of court room advocacy, such as coaching witnesses to lie or sequestering exculpatory evidence, which violate due process.

If a prosecutor participates in a police raid or arrest which later turns out to be illegal, they can also be sued. (See *McSurely v. McClelland*, 694 F2d 309 D.C. Cir. 1982).

Generally qualified immunity is available when government officials may have violated a right, but the right asserted by the plaintiff was not clearly established at the time the acts complained of were committed. The Court looks to the "state of the law" and decides whether an objectively reasonable official should have known that the conduct engaged in was unconstitutional.

Actual government entities or departments alone are not easily sued. Certain immunity doctrines and theories shield government organizations time after time in court; your most vulnerable defendants will be individual bureaucrats and police who commit a wrongful act. Courts have held cities to be not liable for police misconduct, except in such situations where they can be found to have negligently hired, trained, supervised or retianed the errant officer on the payroll after it was foreseeable that he would do something wrong.

Use the various state freedom of information acts to request information about yourself from the various government agencies whom you have been in conflict with. This is a possible way of finding evidence which might be useful at trial.

Rarely will government entities settle. Too often, they will lead a pro-se litigant on to believing that a claim will be settled, hoping he will wait until the statute of limitations is expired.

If you have a strong case for damages, such as loss of property or personal injuries, you may want to consult with an attorney who is an expert in civil rights litigation before proceeding pro-se. Some might work on a contingent fee basis.

Federal courts may exercise what is called "pendant jurisdiction" in civil rights cases, which permit you to join claims under state law in federal court. If you are bringing a state claim against a government entity in federal court together with a federal civil rights claim, you must comply with presentment requirements, which require you to send a written claim by certified mail to the appropriate person by statute under a certain time deadline before filing suit. Each state has different rules and it can get tricky.

In a federal civil rights suit, discovery may be the key to making your case viable. Remember the use of interrogatories and requests for documents allowed by the Federal Rules of Civil Procedure.

Be sure to include in your complaint requests for (1) jury trial (2) a claim for compensatory damages, and (3) a claim for punitive damages.

It might be a good idea to ask a local civil rights lawyer to read the complaint and edit it. The complaint is unequivocally the most important document you will file. If it is legally defective or insufficient the entire case may be doomed. Government entities hire lawyers who do nothing all day except defend civil rights claims, and they know every possible defense to raise, and even if their client's conduct is indefensible, they will still defend it.

Prison Litigation Reform Act

Voltaire is said to have remarked that we can tell much about a society from the way it treats its prisoners. In fact, we can also learn much more about a society that limits the rights of prisoners to do things about their conditions through legal process. Congress has done precisely that. It has passed a bill known as the Prison Litigation Reform Act to place obstacles to one of the most helpless and dependent classes of people, the prisoners, and placed a sereis of hurdles before them to limit and intimidate them from exercising their basic constuitutional right of access to the court.

For example, prisoners have to exhaust administrative grievance procedures prior to bringing a claim in court. Prison authorities often make it extremely difficult for a prisoner to learn about or to exercise his grievance administratively, and prisoners often never even learn the results of their grievance or learn it after an exceedingly long period has passed.

If a lawsuit has been filed by a prisoner and is deeemd to be frivolous or harrassing, prison authorities can take away time credit for early release on good behavior. Since it is the prison authorities being sued, this indeed puts them in a conflict situation.

While most indigent people are exempt from paying suit fees, prisoners, who earn a few cents a day as virtual slaves in jail, are required to pay over their meager earnings for filing fees.

While in jail, prioners are extorted by guards, set up for gang rapes, beaten by guards, deprived of medical care and occasionally driven to suicide or murdered by other prisoners with the contrivance of guards, and others.

With the Prison Litigation Reform Act, the prison authorities have been given a pass from Congress to engage in further abuses of inmates with less and less accountability.

Almost no lawyers will represent prionsers because of the risk of malpractice from the complex procedural hurdles in suing the prison. Without justice, the prisoners will likely leave jail embittered further and angry at society as never before.

Chapter 10

Suing Your Federal Government For Civil Rights Violations

On the occasion of the 200th anniversary of the *Bill Of Rights*, many attorneys may not realize that these rights each contain within them an intrinsic enabling authority for the purpose of redressing violations of these rights by those federal employees entrusted to uphold and protect them.

It is worth remembering that the authors of the *Bill Of Rights* were heavily influenced by Anglo-Saxon legal theorists such as Sir William Blackstone, who declared that there were "three absolute rights... the right of personal security, the right of personal liberty and the right of personal property.(1) Blackstone believed the principal aim of society is to protect individuals in the enjoyment of these absolute rights which were vested in them by the immutable laws of nature.(2)

Blackstone's ideas became embodied in the Federalist papers, and in the writings of James Madison on property interests, which he defined in quite broad terms:

> In its larger and juster meaning, it embraces every thing to which a man may attach a value and have a right, and *which leaves to every one else the like advantage...* [A] man has a property in his opinions, and the free communication of them. He has a property of peculiar value in his religious opinions, and in the profession and practice dictated by them. He has a property very dear to him in the safety and liberty of his person. He has an equal property in the free use of his faculties, and free choice of the objects on which to employ them.
>
> "The protection of these faculties," Madison wrote in *The Federalist* No. 10, "is the first object of government."

As Madison might have anticipated, and as modern students of law and history may realize, in the pursuit of its various other objectives, the federal government from time to time treads on these rights and "faculties" and on the natural rights of mankind, whose protection is found in the Ninth Amendment of the U.S. Constitution.

When Congress enacted Title 42 U.S. Code § 1983 and other federal civil rights laws for the redress of violations of these rights, it did not extend liability to federal officials and employees. Instead, these laws were held to apply to "state action," and the actions of county and municipal government (except when federal officials conspired with others). See *Fonda v. Gray,* 1983(CA 9) CAL 707 F.2d. 435.

The dilemma on how to obtain compensation for victims of "constitutional torts" by federal actors remained essentially unresolved until the case of *Bivens v. Six Unknown Narcotics Agents,* 403 U.S. 388 (1971).

Bivens has had more impact on the accountability of federal government officials than perhaps any other decision in the history of American law. The central issue in *Bivens* was whether the Fourth Amendment of the Federal constitution created an implied right of action. This was decided affirmatively in a claim for damages by individuals whose home was searched unreasonably (and hence unconstitutionally) by federal narcotic agents. Jurisdiction was not claimed under Title 42 U.S. Code § 1983, which as of this writing, has not yet been held to extend liability to federal officials, in most circumstances. Instead, the enabling legislation was found under Title 28 U.S. Code § 1331, which grants general jurisdiction on the basis of a federal question.

Subsequent cases have held the *Bivens* theory of recovery applies to other claims under the various rights enumerated in the Constitution. (For decisions concerning redress of Fifth Amendment claims with *Bivens* actions, see *Young v. Pierce*, (DC Tex. 544 F.Supp. 1010) and Eighth Amendment claims *Mackey v. Indiana Hospital,* (DC PA 562 F.Supp. 1251[(3)]).

Litigants who seek to bring claims against federal officials for abuses of their authority have been confused concerning the proper way to characterize their actions in the pleadings. Generally speaking, how one drafts a complaint, and not what evidence is to be introduced, determines whether a claim can survive as a federal cause of action. *Tully v. Mott Supermarkets, Inc.,* 337 F.Supp. 834, 844 D.N.J. (1972).

For example, cases have held that if other theories of recovery are pleaded, a *Bivens* action must fail. This has forced attorneys to select whether they wish to use the Federal Tort Claims Act (Title 28 U.S. Code § 2679) and its strict presentment requirements and other federal law, or to rely on a *Bivens* theory. A complaint alleging both theories is at risk of a dispositive motion. *Serra v. Pichardo,* 786 F.2d. 237 (6th Cir.).

Another easy mistake to make is in deciding who to name as a defendant. A lawsuit naming the FBI or United States Department of Justice, per se, as defendants may fail because the agencies are likely to raise certain immunity defenses which have yet to be abolished.

Federal employees may become personally liable for constitutional deprivation by direct participation, failure to remedy wrongs after learning about it, creation of a policy or custom under which constitutional practices occur or gross negligence in managing subordinates who cause violations. (*Gallegos v. Haggerty, Norther District of New York,* 689 F.Supp. 93)

Although certain federal officials have absolute immunity from private suit, most executive officials enjoy only qualified immunity. The rationale for the distinction is that higher officials require greater liability than officials with less complex and discretionary responsibilities. *(Hatori v. Haya,* 751 F.Supp. 1401.)

Any action is considered to be against the "sovereign" and hence fails to state a claim if judgment would "interfere with public administration, or compel the United States to act in foreign policy, or enjoin foreign policy." (*Sanchez Espinola v. Reagan,* 770 F.2d. 202, *Rochfort v. Gibbs,* 696 F.Supp. 1151, WD Michigan, 1988).

Many litigants facing civil lawsuits in which the United States is the plaintiff have erroneously sought to counterclaim against the U.S. The United States, however, to this date has not waived sovereign immunity for claims for damages, (see *United States v. Northside Realty Associates*, 324 F.Supp. 287, 291 (N.D. GA 1971) dismissing a counterclaim asserted against the Attorney General, where plaintiff in the suit was the United States on the ground that although the suit was initiated by the Attorney General, the real party in interest was the United States.

When lawsuits are brought against federal officials, they must be brought against them in their "individual" capacity, not their official capacity. The theory appears to be that when federal officials perpetrate constitutional torts, they do so *ultra vires* and lose the shield of sovereign immunity. *Williamson v. U.S. Department of Agriculture,* 815 F.2d. 369, *ACLU Foundation v. Barr,* 952 F.2d. 457, 293 U.S. App. DC 101, (CA DC 1991).

Bivens actions, again, are by no means an exclusive remedy for redressing abuses of authority by federal government employees, even in a political context. In the celebrated case of *Socialist Workers Party v. Attorney General,* 596 F.2d. 58 (1979), 444 U.S. 903 (1979) (cert. denied) one of the many claims of the plaintiff, a Trotskyite communist organization, was for 193 surreptitious entries or burglaries committed by the F.B.I.. Another set of claims was for the use of disruptive informants in the organization, which successfully proved itself to be a non-violent, educational group more involved in promoting and discussing ideas rather than in any violent act.

Judge Thomas Griesa's final decision in the case allowed recovery under the Federal Tort Claims Act for the intentional torts of invasion of privacy for the use of informants as well as for the F.B.I.'s burglaries, under a theory of trespass. Many other counts were dismissed in the case for failure to adhere to the procedural requirements of the Federal Tort Claims Act (FTCA).

Why plaintiff's counsel selected the FTCA rather than the Bivens theory of recovery is not known.

The social consequences of having available remedies such as Bivens and the FTCA are significant. Together with the Freedom of Information Act, The Privacy Act, and the willingness of disillusioned persons within government to act as "whistleblowers," a limited deterrent effect exists to serious violations of civil rights by government.

The sensation caused by the illegal federally sponsored research experiments on mentally disabled children sequestered for nearly 40 years and revealed only recently, indicates the changes in public sentiments.

Nevertheless, many courts have considered civil rights claims to be "disfavored actions." Consider the court in *Littleton v. Berbling,* 468 F.2d. 390 (7th Cir. 1971):

The civil damages suit is worthless, especially if the victim of oppression is a social misfit or an unsavory character.

The words of Justice Louis Brandeis however, offer another view:

Decency, security and liberty alike demand that government officials shall be subjected to the rules of conduct that are commands to the citizen. In a government of laws, existence of the government of laws, existence of the government will be imperiled, if it fails to observe the law scrupulously. Our government is the potent, omnipresent teacher. For good or for ill, it teaches the whole people by its example. Crime is contagious. If the government becomes a lawbreaker, it breeds contempt for the law, it invites every man to come a law unto himself. It invites anarchy. (*United States v. Olmstead*, 277 U.S. 438 (1928).

1. Unfinished Business: A Civil rights Strategy For America's Third Century. Clint Bolick Pacific Research Institute For Public Policy, San Francisco, CA 1990.
2. id.
3. First Amendment litigation concerning IRS tax exempt status for minority political and religious movements is also common. For a historical perspective see Income Disadvantages of Political Activities, (Colum. L. Rev. 273 (1957). Also, Clark, The Limitation On Political Activities; A Discordant Note In the Law Of Charities 46 VA L.Rev. 439 (1960). See also, Communist Party v. Commissioner of Internal Revenue, 332 F.2d. 325, 329(D.C. Cir. 1964; Wolfe v. U.S. Tax Court, (1981) (D.C. Colo. 513 F.Supp. 912.

Chapter 11

Suing Judges

The previous edition of this book, following the lead in the famous Supreme Court case of *Pulliam v. Allen*, 466 US 522 (1984), made available a template for lawsuits against judges.

Subsequent legislation and decisions have made this pretty much an exercise in futility. The so-called Federal Courts Improvement Act of 1996 created so much obfuscation and further challenge to such lawsuits that the chances for such actions to ever succeed are extremely remote.

In fact, our review of reported cases in Lexis has not turned up any successful lawsuits against judges. But nevertheless, some readers have enjoyed a strategic benefit by suing judges and then obtaining the judge's disqualification, which is, of course, a major benefit when you have a hostile judge.

Under the Pulliam decision, litigants were able to sue a judge for what is called **declaratory relief** or **injunctive relief.**

Declaratory relief in the context of a suit against a judge would ask for the Court to give an opinion as to the constitutionality of certain practices or a decision.

Injunctive relief would seek an order commanding the judge to cease and desist the practice, or to implement a corrective practice. Even despite the most serious of circumstances, these lawsuits are not being allowed to go forward, so I believe that to encourage the reader would not be prudent. Except one thing.

While Bar rules do not even allow lawyers to sue judges for the sole purpose of getting them to disqualify themselves, laypersons can do this, with only a very slight risk that they will be sanctioned for so doing. There are also actions in what is called "mandamus" in which judges can be asked to disqualify themselves. (Appendix D).

But Pulliam is dead. There are possible loopholes in the Federal Courts Improvement Act of 1996 to bring lawsuits. A careful reading of Title 42 U.S. Code Section 1983 seems to indicate that if a declaratory decree was violated, only then is injunctive releif available. But apparently suits in the nature of declaratory relief are still possible, though we know of none that have been successful in many, many years.

Chapter 12

How to Sue a Prosecutor Without Hiring a Lawyer

Have you been the victim of a malicious prosecution?

Have government lawyers lied and coaxed witnesses to lie?

Has suspicious evidence appeared out of nowhere to be used in a frame up against you or somebody you care about? Did your fingerprints turn up on something you never touched? Do witnesses say they met you when you never met them? Don't be shocked. This is the New World Order, and many innocent people will be prosecuted for things they never had the remotest connection to.

You have a constitutional right under the Fifth and Fourteenth Amendments to be free from malicious prosecution. That is, trying to convict you of a crime for no good reason.

Unfortunately, some cops and prosecutors do not see it that way. For years prosecutors were immune from suit for malicious prosecution. They were free to run amok over the rights of citizens with little fear of reprisal. Prosecutors have been known to extort favors, ranging from money to sex to political influence in exchange for going easy on a defendant. It is a career that attracts the most ambitious power seekers, Janet Reno, Ted Kennedy, Thomas Dewey, Robert Dole, Arlen Specter, all of these folks had careers as a prosecutor at one time or another. Did I leave out Geraldo Rivera? Yes, Geraldo Rivera too, was a prosecutor, right nearby in Cambridge, Massachusetts, before he realized that he could go further in the media.

Recently a prosecutor was caught going too far. He was caught violating the confidentiality of grand jury proceedings, coaxing witnesses and generally acting recklessly and maliciously in prosecuting somebody who was eventually acquitted. (Appendix.E, Appellate Decision)

But instead of picking on a poor uneducated person he prosecuted a wealthy business executive who knew enough to hire the very best lawyers. This prosecutor's error did not help his career.

The result was a decision in the second highest court in the land eroding a long and rotten tradition of prosecutorial immunity. Moore v. Valder is found in this book as well as the complaint. Refer to Appendix F. It is a Bivens action rather than a suit under Title 42 U.S. Code Section 1983. The latter is a suit which could be brought against state, county or municipal prosecutors. The Valder case is a claim against federal employees so it was required to be a Bivens action, that is a case arising directly from a violation of the Constitution and against a federal official.

As a practical consideration, very few lawyers will be willing to sue prosecutors, even if you pay them hourly. In most cases, if you want to sue a prosecutor, you'll have to do it yourself.

This means you want to file a complaint; and serve it on the prosecutor you are suing as well as other required parties. Procedural rules require you to serve the Attorney General of the United States, if you are suing a federal prosecutor and the Attorney General of the state if you are suing a municipal, state or county prosecutor.

What goes into a complaint?

First, you have to identify the court and you have to identify the parties. Be sure to put the words Complaint and Jury Demand on the caption. Explain the jurisdictional basis of your complaint and your basis for your claim of venue. The Valder case herein has a descriptive introductory paragraph explaining what the case is about. The legal enabling authority is in fact the various amendments of the U.S. Constitution, but the jurisdictional basis is also statutory, governing claims against all federal employees (Title 28 Section 1331).

Most importantly, your complaint has to tell a story, putting the factual description of the events into a format that has become a convention among lawyers and litigants and which will be obvious when you read the accompanying complaint.

Which amendments of the Constitution apply to which kinds of conduct?

Unreasonable search and seizure, false arrest... **FOURTH AMENDMENT**.
Intimidating a person from expressing an opinion... **FIRST AMENDMENT**.
Unfair, illegal conduct affecting integrity of judicial system, malicious prosecutorial conduct, withholding exculpatory evidence... **FIFTH AMENDMENT**.

Simultaneously with serving the complaint it is a good idea to serve discovery pleadings. These are documents which demand documents and answers to written questions in accordance with the rules of court. See Rule 33 of the Federal Rules of Civil Procedure and Rule 34 FRCP.

FRCP Rule 33 allows service of interrogatories (questions in writing requiring answers under oath in writing).

You just cannot ask any question. The question you ask or documents you request must be related to the production of evidence which would be admissible at trial.

You may also ask for admissions to statements. See Rule 36 of the Federal Rules of Civil Procedure.

Rule 64 allows you to try to freeze the assets of the defendants. This can be done by a Motion For Real Estate Attachment. Generally, if your state court will allow a Pre-trial Attachment, your federal court will also.

Read Rule 64 carefully. If you file a Motion For Real Estate Attachment, be sure to include an affidavit and copy of the deed to the prosecutor's property. This can usually be found in the Registry of Deeds.

Without equivocation, you must obtain a copy of the Federal Rules of Civil Procedure.

This will explain the various rules of practices which govern the adjudication of cases in the United States District Court. You may want to amend pleadings, implead new defendants, compel discovery (very often the defendants will give you a hard time about producing documents or answering interrogatories.)

You should also obtain a copy of Black's Law Dictionary. You must learn the jargon or forget litigating.

At some point in time, if your case survives motions to dismiss, you will have a pretrial conference and get sent to trial. Before that time, contact your local federal bookstore and order a copy of the Federal Rules of Evidence. For about $6.00 you can learn how the hearsay rule works, what kind of questions may or may not be asked, how to introduce evidence and other similar topics.

But before you get to that stage, the opposition will try to terminate your case with a motion for summary judgment or judgment on the pleadings. It is up to you to familiarize yourself with Rule 56 of the Federal Rules of Civil Procedure. And read the Valder case carefully.

It is up to you to prove that your fact pattern in your situation is closely analogous to the Valder case. In such an event, you should be able to show that outside of the courtroom, the prosecutor abused his authority and deviated from the bounds of acceptable standards of conduct within the profession.

This might mean: suppressing evidence
coaching witnesses to lie
misleading the grand jury
breaching confidential testimony before grand jury
producing false documents

You must show, if faced with a summary judgment motion, that facts are in dispute and that at as a matter of law, based on the Valder precedent, the case should go forward.

Once you get to trial, you have to put on witnesses to prove that the government's lawyer had no probable cause to proceed against you, that he engaged in unethical or overreaching conduct, that you are innocent (preferably had already been found innocent by a jury or judge) and that you suffered damages, i.e. false imprisonment, loss of earnings, humiliation, emotional distress and what have you.

But more importantly, you must prove under Valder, that the prosecutor did things in the <u>investigation and preparation</u> of the case that violated your due process rights.

Chapter 13

How to Sue City Hall Without a Lawyer

Have you been wronged by actions of a municipality (i.e. city, town or village)? Perhaps a Zoning Board won't let you put a sign on your lawn. Or a Building Inspector won't leave you alone. Maybe the local police have a grudge against you and you can't get around town without being followed, stopped, frisked and cited. You might own land you can't build on. There are dozens of scenarios that invite pro-se litigants to seek federal intervention through civil rights statutes that were meant to protect your constitutional rights from abuses of government authority.

Title 42 U.S. Code § 1983 is perhaps the leading enabling statute to allow you to file lawsuits against municipal officials, employees, and occasionally municipalities themselves.

The statute reads as follows: Every person who, under color of any statute ordinance, regulation, custom, or usage, of any State or Territory, subjects, or causes to be subjected, any citizen of the United States or other person within the jurisdiction thereof to the deprivation of any rights, privileges, or immunities secured by the Constitution and laws, shall be liable to the party injured in an action at law, suit in equity, or other proper proceeding for redress.

Understanding your Constitutional rights is a vital pre-requisite to filing suit under the statute. Read the Bill of Rights very carefully as well as the rest of the Constitution. Due Process and equal protection issues raise themselves over and over again every time a local politician or bureaucrat acts maliciously to a local resident. Due Process is the right to an opportunity to be heard, and notice of that opportunity. It is guaranteed by the Fifth and Fourteenth Amendment of the United States Constitution. Some case citations which explain due process include: *Application of Gault*, 87 Supreme Court Reporter, 1428, 1435; *Schneider v. Margossian*, 349 F.Supp. 741; *Pinsky v. Duncan*, 898 F2d 852; *Boddie v. Connecticut*, 91 S.Ct. 780.

Violations of due process are violations of a federal right and, in theory, at least, can or should invoke federal jurisdiction.

The Equal Protection clause of the Fourteenth Amendment guarantees the right of people to be free from arbitrary discrimination, especially but not exclusively on the basis of race, religion, national origin, gender, handicap, sexual preference, political views or even just because one is unpopular at City Hall for example, or not liked by neighbors. The key to the concept is that similarly situated people must be treated the same way by public servants. See *Yick Wo v. Hopkins*, 118 U.S. 356, which held "state laws must be applied fairly, not with a heavy hand and evil eye." This case derived from a municipal ordinance governing the laundry business which was enforced against Asians but not Caucasians.

The First Amendment guarantees you the right to express your opinions, to form groups to express your opinions, to practice any religion or no religion and to be free from religious coercion.

The Second Amendment permits gun ownership. Of course many government restrictions exist on gun ownership, but restrictions must have a rational relationship to a compelling public interest, otherwise they might be subject to Constitutional challenge.

The Fourth Amendment covers the right to be free from unreasonable search and seizure. It has been whittled down substantially by the U.S. Supreme Court for the sake of the War On Drugs. The Fourth Amendment is what requires police to obtain a warrant before entering your home and also protects you from an illegal arrest.

The Fifth Amendment, in summary, covers your right to avoid self-incriminating statements. (As a practical matter it means that you can keep silent when asked about a crime unless you are given immunity). It also means that you have the right to due process of law before any deprivation of your life, liberty and property, can occur. It is often used to challenge zoning board decisions.

The Sixth Amendment provides you the right to legal counsel in criminal prosecutions when your liberty is at stake, and the right to confront witnesses.

The Seventh Amendment allows you the right to a trial according to common law in the federal courts. This basically means that the law used to decide your case will be derived from legal principles set down in other cases which were decided at any time between the original common law of medieval England up until the day before your trial.

The Eighth Amendment, in theory, protects you from excessive bail, exorbitant fines and cruel and unusual punishment. Nevertheless, forfeiture laws, million dollar bail requirements and beatings of prisoners are rampant in our society.

The Ninth Amendment is perhaps the most under utilized part of the Bill of Rights. It allows the people to assert every other "natural right," common law right, and reasonably expected right and freedom that the Constitution does not explicitly cover.

Privacy rights, the right to be free from excessive regulation of one's affairs are examples of rights protected by the Ninth Amendment.

The Thirteenth Amendment covers the right to be free from involuntary servitude. It is used to protect minorities who are discriminated against in entering contracts. It has also been used in regard to religious cults who have intimidated and exploited their members.

The Fourteenth Amendment is, as mentioned above, a protection against state deprivation of due process and equal protection.

The violation of any of these rights by employees or officials of a city or town may be grounds for a lawsuit that you can bring yourself, without hiring a lawyer.

And you need not exhaust your state remedies before bringing suit under Title 42 U.S. Code 1983. (See *Monroe v. Pape*, 365 U.S. 167 (1961)).

Suing the city under the civil rights laws is a distinct action from the one against its employees.

A body of law has developed making civil rights lawsuits against municipalities disfavored actions. However, it is another issue to sue the city for negligent training, supervision and hiring of an employee who does something wrong.

Some states require a specified kind of claim letter prior to bringing a lawsuit against a municipality. Research this under the topic of "**Presentment**" in the index to your state statutes; you may also check under "**Notice**," "**Actions**" or other headings.

After proper presentment is given and the time waiting period elapses... (you must time this in accord with local rules on limitations of actions), then you file a complaint in your local U.S. District Court. This is a legal pleading which identifies all parties and clearly describes the problem. Although lawyers have a distinct advantage through training in drafting a complaint, the law helps pro-se litigants overcome the hurdles. A complaint may not be dismissed on motion if it states some sort of claim, baseless though it may be proved to be and inartistically as the complaint may be drawn. This is particularly true where the Plaintiff is not represented by counsel. Brooks v. Pennsylvania Railroad Co. 91 F. Supp. 101 (SDNY 1950)

The Federal Rules of Civil Procedure explain how to write a complaint.

Rules 8(a) and 10 govern complaints. Every pleading shall contain a caption setting forth the name of the court, the title of the pleading, i.e. ("complaint").

Your complaint must include a statement of where jurisdiction is derived from, a description of the claim, and a demand for judgment for the relief to which you deem yourself entitled, such as money damages, an injunction, costs, interests, declaratory judgment on other relief.

A hypothetical complaint is printed below.

UNITED STATES DISTRICT COURT
DISTRICT OF MASSACHUSETTS

CIVIL DOCKET NO.

VANNA VICTIM, Plaintiff	)))	
v.	)	**COMPLAINT AND JURY DEMAND**
JOE DOE, and TOWN OF DANA, Defendants	)))))	

JURISDICTION

This action is brought under Title 42 U.S.C. § 1983.

1. Plaintiff Vanna Victim, a natural person, resides at 330 Dartmouth Street in the Town of Dana, Neversink County, Massachusetts. She represents herself pro-se.

2. Defendant Joe Doe, is a resident of the Town of Dana. He is employed by the Town of Dana as a law enforcement officer

3. Defendant Town of Dana is a municipal corporation in Neversink County, Massachusetts.

4. Plaintiff at all times relevant hereto was a member of the Committee For A Better Town. In her activities she appeared on local television programs, wrote letters to the local press and organized pickets in from of Town Hall.

5. Plaintiff's expressed opinions were highly critical of the Chief of Police of Dana, the Board of Selectmen and the Zoning Board of Appeals.

6. Nevertheless, these opinions were protected by the First Amendment of the Federal Constitution.

7. On February 19, 1994 the Plaintiff organized a picket line to protest the lack of honesty, openness and accountability in Dana Town Hall.

8. Defendant Joe Doe approached the picket line and advised Plaintiff she was “making enemies in Town Hall” and that “serious consequences would follow this.”

9. The following day the Plaintiff was pulled over and arrested for passing through a stop sign. Subsequently at a jury trial she was acquitted.

10. On March 14, 1994, the Plaintiff was pulled over by Defendant Doe and arrested for speeding. She was acquitted at jury trial.

11. On March 21, 1994 the Plaintiff was informed her assessment on her home would increase by 40%.

12. She ultimately contested this and was successful on appeal.

13. Repeatedly, Plaintiff received harassing phone calls on her phone, which rang once and stopped at 3:00 a.m. in the morning each night for several weeks.

14. Caller ID and a telephone trap ultimately revealed them to be from Defendant John Doe.

15. At all times relevant hereto the Plaintiff enjoyed a right under the First Amendment of the federal constitution to express opinions and peacefully assemble in protest of municipal policies.

16. The Defendants illegally chilled Plaintiff's First Amendment rights by using the above described threats and intimidation to frighten her from expressing constitutionally protected opinions, in violation of Title 42 U.S. Code § 1983.

17. Plaintiff was damaged thereby.

COUNT TWO

18. Defendant Town of Dana owed a duty of reasonable care to its residents in hiring, training and supervising its personnel.

19. Defendant Town of Dana negligently breached its duty by hiring, poorly training and poorly supervising Defendant Doe.

20. As a direct and proximate cause of the negligence of the Town of Dana, the Plaintiff suffered great pain of mind and was intimidated from expressing her opinions. She eventually was required to travel out of state and required psychiatric counseling.

Wherefore Plaintiff prays this Court:

(a) Award Plaintiff such damages as a jury of her peers deems appropriate and just.
(b) Costs of litigation.
(c) Interests as provided by statute.
(d) A permanent injunction against Defendants, their agents, servants or employees enjoining them from harassing, intimidating or threatening Plaintiff.

JURY TRIAL DEMANDED

Respectfully submitted,

____

Vanna Victim
Plaintiff Pro-Se
Plaintiff's Address
City, State, Zip Code
Telephone:
Date:

Chapter 14

The Seventh Amendment

The federal constitution recognizes the importance of the common law, derived from the Anglo Saxon body of jurisprudence, and the fundamental right to a jury trial, which was recognized in the Magna Carta. This dates to the thirteenth century and empowered English subjects with the kinds of guarantees of individual liberty and property rights which were also demanded by the Founding Fathers.

The Seventh Amendment provides: "In suits at common law, where the value in controversies shall exceed twenty dollars, the right of trial by jury shall be preserved."

The amendment is now widely used to restrict the access of citizens to jury trials. For example, bankruptcy courts are not courts at common law but at equity. In *Katchen vs. Landy*, 382 U.S. 323, the United States Supreme Court held that a bankruptcy judge could make decisions regarding the setting aside of a debtor's conveyance (known as a voidable preference) on the grounds that a "bankruptcy court was a court of equity and constituted a forum before which a jury would be out of place and would go far to dismantle the statutory scheme."

In decisions regarding the power of administrative agencies to exercise jurisdiction in tribunals or in court actions, the Supreme Court has in effect decided that a jury trial is "incompatible with the whole concept of administrative jurisdiction." (See *Block vs. Hirsh*, 256 U.S. 135) In fact, the reasoning goes further that the administrative agencies did not exist in the days in which common law was originated, therefore cases involving administrative law and administrative procedure need not be adjudicated by a jury.

The Seventh Amendment has been interpreted to hold that original determination of where federal rights should be decided belongs to Congress but that the Supreme Court has the final say. (See *Crowell vs. Benson*, 285 U.S. 22).

The Supreme Court of Rhode Island has made distinctions in the nature of the kinds of actions brought by an administrative agency. In *Cambio vs. Bendick*, (558 A 2d 941), Justice Weisberger held that a landowner was entitled to a jury trial with respect to the Department of Environmental Management's claim for civil penalties but not for its claims that it was entitled injunctive relief and that a consent order had been violated. The latter, the court held, was analogous to a civil contempt and need not be adjudicated by a jury. However, the agency's action to collect statutory penalties against a landowner was analogous to a common law action for debt, and gave the citizen the right to trial on issues of both liability and damages, even though a claim for injunctive relief was combined in the suit.

When one appears in a federal hearing, for example in a Social Security matter or a decision making board of the Federal Communications Commission, there is no recognized right to a jury trial simply because these are not common law actions. Neither social security nor electronic communications even existed when the founding fathers adopted the Seventh Amendment.

As a practical matter, the administrative agencies shift power away from courts and the public and into unelected, and unaccountable appointees who staff these bureaus. Although these bureaucracies wield tremendous power over the public, it is incredibly costly and very difficult to bring a case to review their decisions in court.

The standard of "judicial review" is generally to determine if the actions of the agency violated the law. New evidence is generally not admissible. If an agency acted arbitrarily or capriciously or engaged in a violation of constitutional rights that was sufficiently egregious to attract the court's attention, perhaps the agency's actions would be overturned. Unfortunately, the most that would likely happen is that the case would be sent back to the agency for further proceedings.

Little hope exists that the real issue of the constitutionality of these agencies and the routine damage that they do will ever be challenged by the federal court system.

The prevailing judicial philosophy is that administrative agencies and the rules and regulations that they enforce are in fact "new statutory public rights created by Congress" (*Atlas Roofing Co. vs. Occupational Safety and Health Review Commission*, 518 F2d. 990, cert. granted U.S. Supreme Court Docket 75-746 and 75-748) In the same case, Mr. Justice White said "Congress is not required by the Seventh Amendment to choke the already crowded federal courts with new types of litigation or prevented from committing some new types of litigation to administrative agencies with special competence in the relevant field. This is the case even if the Seventh Amendment would have required a jury where the adjudication of those rights is assigned to a federal court instead of an administrative agency."

Thus the reasoning behind the Supreme Court's decision denying a claim under the Sixth Amendment that the assessment and adjudication of tax penalties could not be made without a jury even though tax collection was a part of common law litigation historically. In *Helvering vs. Mitchell*, 303 U.S. 391, the Court decided that the "determination of the facts upon which (tax) liability is based may be made by an administrative agency instead of a jury."

The role of a jury to decide the facts in a case, the judge to decide the law and the independence of the judiciary from the Executive Branch of government is all blurred when one becomes involved in an administrative proceeding.

The administrative agency is a part of the Executive Branch of government, and it is both judge and jury. It interprets its own rules and regulations in many instances, even if a civil service "administrative law" judge is called in to hear your case.

Lawyers have developed administrative law as a specialty in itself. Many lawyers who practice before administrative agencies were formerly employees of the agency, although they usually wait a year or two to avoid impropriety. Sometimes lawyers who practice in Washington, DC before administrative agencies command fees as much as $750.00 per hour.

One may reasonably speculate whether the huge commercial enterprises who pay these fees are paying for legal expertise or access to power.

Simply put, we must find a way to change the way federal judges become federal judges. That is, they should be elected by the people, at every level, from the U.S. District Court all the way to the Supreme Court. Similarly, in those states like the author's own state of Massachusetts, the legislature must be told that we want the right to vote on who our judges will be. We should be able to vote judges out of office, organize recall petitions or have impeachment proceedings against them initiated by petition.

There is no rational reason why judges should be appointed for life. This would seem to only foster disregard for the public good. Worse, what we see in the courts now is “groupthink,” a view that fosters the illusion that administrative law creates “public rights.” It's frightening.

A creative lawsuit might be one brought against a federal official engaging in administrative action against you in which you request and are denied a jury trial. You could bring a Bivens action, i.e. a lawsuit based directly on the violation of a constitutional right, against the federal employee for violation of your Seventh Amendment right. Unfortunately, based on the judicial philosophies now prevalent in the federal courts, such a suit would be deemed frivolous and you could be fined by the Court (without a jury trial!) for even bringing the lawsuit. It's called a “sanction” and the enabling authority for it is found in Rule 11 of the Federal Rules of Civil Procedure. Pro-se litigants as well as lawyers can be sanctioned. In Boston, a law firm was once sanctioned for $45,000.00 for bringing a frivolous lawsuit.

The best thing to do if you are faced with an administrative proceeding against you is to learn the administrative law and procedure you are being faced with well. If you hire a lawyer, find a specialist in the particular field of administrative law you are dealing with. The Code of Federal Regulation covers these topics, and each agency will ordinarily give you copies of its substantive and procedural laws.

When you show up for your hearing, don't expect a jury trial.

Chapter 15

Due Process

Legal scholars have divided the concept of due process into two varieties. Procedural due process is better known and understood. It generally refers to the opportunity to be heard, notice, the right to a meaningful hearing and the other aspects of what happens in a case before the courts reach its decision.

Less known and less understood is the concept of Substantive Due Process. A well established body of law exists to show how the Fourteenth Amendment's Due Process Clause recognizes a number of rights, which limit the conduct of the state (or municipal or county governments) vis a vis we the people.

District Judge Hull of the Northeastern District of the U.S, District Court of Tennessee is quoted at 592 F. Supp. 776 as describing Substantive Due Process as follows:

> These rights have been found either specifically or by implication in the Bill of Rights and the "privileges and immunities" clause of the Fourteenth Amendment. For example, as citizens, we enjoy a substantive right to pass freely from state to state, to carry on interstate commerce, to contract, to own property, to engage in life's common occupations, to acquire useful knowledge, to marry and rear children, to worship God according to the dictates of conscience, to be free from illegal searches and seizures of our persons, and to be free from unnecessary violence at the hands of law enforcement officers. The due process clause has been found to protect the sanctity of the person and the family from arbitrary and irrational state actions which abridge these fundamental rights and "shock the conscience."

An example of the kind of state bullying the Fourteenth Amendment seeks to prevent was found in the case of *Wilson v. Taylor*, 773 F2d 1539 (1984). A Florida police officer fired for dating the daughter of a felon was able to recover for violation of his due process rights. The court held that a state violates the Fourteenth Amendment when it seeks to interfere with a social relationship of two or more people.

In *Rochin v. California* it was held that:

> Substantive Due Process rights involves those claims where, although no provision of the Bill of Rights is implicated, the state's conduct is such so as to shock the conscience of the court and thus violate the Due Process Clause. (See 342 U.S. 165, 172).

"Due Process of law is a summarized constitutional guarantee of respect for those personal immunities which, as Justice Cardozo wrote, are "so rooted in the tradition and conscience of our people as to be ranked fundamental." (*Snyder v. Massachusetts*, 291 U.S. 97), or implicit in the concept of ordered liberty (*Polko v. State*, 302 U.S. 319).

Said Justice Blackman, "I also do not understand the court to intimate that the sole content of the Due Process is procedural regularity. I continue to believe that there are certain government actions that, even if undertaken with a full panoply of procedural protection, are in and of themselves, antithetical to fundamental motions of due process."

Procedural Due Process

Procedural Due Process protects your opportunity to be heard at a meaningful time and a meaningful place, promoting fairness in dispute resolution. *Fuentes v. Shevin*, 407 U.S. 67. Procedural due process involves guarantees that there will be no deprivation of your right to life, liberty or property without a hearing which you have notice of, and an opportunity to be heard.

Property interests include any "legitimate claim of entitlement" to a benefit. *Board of Regents v. Roth*, 408 U.S. 564 (1972).

State colleges have been a fertile ground for cases involving the rights of students and faculty to hearings governing such matters as suspension, discipline and firing.

In *Dixon v. Alabama State Board of Education*, 294 F2d 150 (5th Cir. 1961) it was held that a student enrolled in a state college has due process rights as to his status as a student, i.e. to determine if she could be suspended. See also *Goss v. Lopez*, 419 U.S. 565 (1975).

Welfare recipients also are entitled to a hearing before they can be terminated from receiving welfare. See *Goldberg v. Kelly*, 397 U.S. 254.

The requirement of notice as an element of procedural due process is clearly described in *Mullane v. Central Hanover Bank & Trust Co.*, 339 U.S. 306 (1950).

The Mullane case strongly criticized publication as a method of "acquiring interested parties of the fact that their rights are before the courts," stated Justice Jackson.

It is not an accident that the greater number of cases reaching this court on the question of adequacy of notice have been concerned with actions founded on process constructively served through local newspapers.

The correct method of satisfying procedural due process requirements includes the use of service of writs by constables or sheriffs, to serve summonses and complaints.

Federal civil cases now permit service by certified mail and provide for a form for acknowledging receipt of service.

The legal history of New York includes the case of *United States v. Brand Jewelers, Inc.*, 318 F. Supp. 1293 (1970). The federal government in the Brand case obtained an injunction against defendant from systematically obtaining default judgments against economically disadvantaged defendants, by utilizing so-called "sewer service" in which process servers pretend to serve papers but instead threw them away and filed phony affidavits claiming that real service was made. A merchant selling goods on "easy credit terms" through door to door salesmen used "sewer service" to routinely collect default judgments against its customers.

The federal government became involved because an ongoing pattern of civil rights violations had been occurring.

Consumer attorney Ralph Nader sponsored an in-depth investigation of Citibanks alleged use of "sewer service" to recover bad loans. According to the report, two Citibank process servers were subjected to Justice Department enforcement actions for breaches of the Soldiers and Sailors Civil Relief Act and the Civil Rights Act. The Soldiers and Sailors Civil Relief Act requires process servers to ensure that the defendant is not in Military Service prior to default.

Briefly summarized, then, "sewer service" is a violation of due process because it deprives the litigant of the opportunity to be heard and notice of a hearing.

Readers of our newsletter know that violations of substantive due process rights give rise to suits under Title 42 U.S. Code Section 1983, a federal civil rights statute, which allows actions against municipal county and state bureaucrats.

Chapter 16

What Is Equal Protection of the Law?

In 1868, the Fourteenth Amendment was added to our Constitution. The legacy of the Fourteenth Amendment's equal protection clause is that all persons are to be treated the same under the law, that all persons are entitled to the same rights, same consideration in judicial proceedings, and to be treated the same way by government, in housing, job opportunities, academic opportunities and access to public accommodations.

As a practical matter, this is more wishful thinking than anything else. Any lawyer who is intellectually honest must admit that some people will be treated better in court or by police because of wealth, status, connections or having a more effective lawyer.

Political correctness, as exemplified by affirmative action, twists and distorts hiring practices, availability of public housing and college admissions, government contracts and more.

Large corporations, such as Denny's and Mitsubishi, have been involved in discrimination cases of tremendous proportions. These are all Fourteenth Amendment issues which invoke the Equal Protection clause.

For the sake of "public policy" economic activity in the United States has been subjected to intervention by the federal courts by those who have been able to persuade decision makers to give preferential treatment to favored groups.

In *Metro Broadcasting v. FCC*, 497 U.S. 547, the United States Supreme Court upheld a Federal Communications Commission policy that gave preferential treatment to certain minority and female applicants for broadcast station licenses. Justice Brennan said this was a lofty ambition of the FCC and upheld it because it contributed to "fostering broadcasting diversity."

Public works contractors have been familiar with requirements that certain jobs be given to "minority" group members, that minority sub-contractors be given contracts and other adjustments be made to give one minority an advantage not shared by other groups to "compensate for past injustices." This has prompted court challenges and legislative attention.

Within the past two years, at least 15 states have proposed laws to repeal affirmative action, and political debates on the subject are intense.

White people, especially white males, are now clearly victims of the denial of equal protection of the law, whenever affirmative action programs give others preferential treatment. Without denying historical mistreatment of women and minorities, there are serious constitutional questions raised by affirmative action.

Lessons for pro-se litigants: If you are a victim of any kind of ethnic or gender discrimination, it is important that you complain immediately to your local state commission against discrimination and the Equal Employment Opportunity Commission, whether you are white, black, yellow or whatever.

Those agencies will conduct at government expense an investigation into the facts of your complaint, and, if they determine you have a case, they will represent you.

If they do not find in your favor, they will notify you of your right to sue, and give you a time limit. Specific civil rights statutes apply, and lawyers exist who will take such cases on a contingency.

In other cases where you can prove that similarly situated people are treated differently for a reason at variance from public policy, the violation of your right to equal protection is still a civil rights violation.

Entire court systems such as the divorce courts engage in discrimination against males in child custody cases. It is possible to bring civil rights lawsuits against state court judges for injunctive relief for violations of Fourteenth Amendment rights under Title 42 U.S. Code Section 1983.

A big hurdle is, federal courts have an "abstention doctrine" based on, among other things, a doctrine known as *comity* or respect for the decisions of other courts.

Abstention and Comity

Abstention simply means federal courts "abstain." Historically, they will not involve themselves in state court domestic relations proceedings because they have determined that the states are a more appropriate forum.

Nevertheless, under Article III, Section 2 of the Constitution, federal courts have jurisdiction when a federal right is affected. They simply decline to exercise it, often to the public detriment.

This often leaves people without an effective remedy in dealing with abuses by the state court system.

In *Younger v. Harris*, 401 U.S. 37 (1971), a federal challenge to a state prosecution was brought by a college professor arrested under a state criminal syndicalism statute for distribution of communist literature. He attempted to obtain injunctive relief against his prosecution, claiming the state law was clearly unconstitutional. He was unsuccessful because of the "abstention" doctrine.

Justice Black explained the court's reason for not getting involved:

> "...the basic doctrine of equity jurisprudence (is) that courts of equity should not act, and particularly should not act to restrain a criminal prosecution, when the moving

party has an adequate remedy at law and will not suffer irreparable injury if denied equitable relief.

The policy of restraining courts of equity from interfering with criminal prosecution is reinforced by an even more vital consideration, the notion of "comity," that is, a proper respect for state functions, a recognizing of the fact that the entire country is made up of a Union of separate state governments, and a continuance of the belief that the National Government will fare best if the States and their institutions are left free to perform their separate functions in their separate ways. This, perhaps for lack of a better and clearer way to describe it, is referred to by many as "Our Federalism." [What] the concept [represents] is a system in which there is sensitivity to the legitimate interests of both State and National Governments, and in which the National Government, anxious through it may be to vindicate and protect federal rights and federal interests, always endeavors to do so in ways that will not unduly interfere with the legitimate activities of the States."

Chapter 17

The Legalized Crime of Zoning

The right to use one's land as one wishes is not recognized as an absolute right by the courts of the United States. If you have ever tried to obtain a zoning variance you will fully understand the significance of this statement.

You might have reasonably expected that your right to use your property as you wished was protected by the Fifth, Ninth and Fourteenth Amendments of the United States Constitution. The Fifth and the Fourteenth govern depriving one of a property right without due process of law. The Ninth Amendment interest in the context of zoning law applies to the natural right of using one's land.

Unfortunately, pure constitutional arguments are unlikely to work in federal court, unless you overcome layers of judicial tests and mechanical applications of a labyrinth of rules and exceptions. In a minority of a few well publicized cases, landowners have been able to sue successfully claiming that the overregulation of their property has been a "taking" without due process of law. (See *Littlefield v. City of Afton*, 785 F2d 596 (8th Cir. 1986).

Federal judges unfortunately have developed a concept known as "qualified immunity," which they hold shields government officials wielding discretionary powers from liability for civil damages insofar as their conduct does not violate clearly established statutory or constitutional rights of which a reasonable person would have known. *Harlow v. Fitzgerald*, 457 U.S. 800 (1982). Even defendants who violate constitutional rights enjoy a qualified immunity, unless it is further demonstrated that their conduct was unreasonable under the applicable standard, *Davis v. Scherer*, 468 U.S. 183 (1984). When the showdown in court comes before a citizen who is hardworking, productive and paying his taxes and perhaps running a business and creating jobs on one hand and a few bureaucratic parasites on the other hand; guess whose side the court is more likely to be on? Most claims never get to the jury. They are dismissed by means of summary judgment or directed verdict.

It gets worse. In *Roy v. Augusta*, 712 F2d 1517, a federal court revealed the policy of shielding zoning boards from review of most of their decisions. This was upheld in *Raskiewicz v. Town of New Boston*, 754 F2d 38 in which it was held: "where the state ... offers a panoply of administrative and judicial remedies, litigants may not ordinarily obtain federal court review of local zoning and planning disputes by means of 42 U.S. Section 1983."

This precedent was used to declare that the failure to permit cross examination of witnesses at a zoning hearing was not a denial of procedural due process. (*Chongris v. Andover Board of Appeals*, 811 F2d 37).

One bright spot: *Nester Colon Media v. Custodio*, 964 F2d 32 (1st Cir.) held that denial of a land use permit in unjustifiable retaliation of an applicant's expression of a political opinion was a violation of the First Amendment.

Nevertheless, most cases reviewed in preparation of this chapter were discouraging. More typical was the holding in *Parrat v. Taylor*, 451 U.S. 527 which held that "not every deprivation of a property interest sinks to the level of a 14th Amendment violation."

Nevertheless, victims of zoning will want to pursue whatever remedy might be available to them. State remedies generally include some form of judicial review of what a board does. Standard arguments revolve around the hardship to a family if a building permit is not allowed. Constitutional challenges frequently point out that the regulatory scheme has no rational relationship to a legitimate government interest, such as health, traffic control or safety.

Towns often allow well connected people who appear with the "right" architects, contractors and lawyers to do things outsiders will not be able to do. Evidence of a pattern of this kind of activity might be admissible to prove a deprivation of equal protection of the law, in violation of the 14th Amendment.

In the case of *Cordeco Development v. Santiago Vasquez*, 539 F2d 256 (1st Cir.) the defendants issued certain permits to members of a politically influential family that owned land adjacent to the plaintiff's, who could not obtain the same permit, even though the circumstances appeared identical in every manner except the identities of the parties. Since *Cordeco*, courts in the First Circuit and many other federal courts have rejected equal protection claims in these kind of fact patterns, although the *Cordeco* plaintiffs prevailed. One holding held that plaintiff's constitutional claims should be rejected because "the dispute was too typical of the sum of the mill dispute between a developer and a town planning agency... to rise to the level of due process violation" *Creative Environments v. Estabrook*, 680 F2d 822 (1st Cir.) This isn't much comfort for property owners.

This observer views this as essentially an abdication of the responsibility of the federal courts to protect the public from governments at the state and municipal level when they trample on the rights of citizens. If they abdicate, who is left?

Chapter 18

Some Federal Decisions Help Pro-se Litigants

If you are a pro-se litigant facing a motion to dismiss because of some real or imagined flaw allegedly found in your complaint, you are not without hope.

We have located four federal decisions which offer you considerable protection. In your opposition to such motions, you may do well to cite these cases:

Picking v. Pennsylvania Railway, (151 F2d. 240) Third Circuit Court of Appeals. In Picking, the plaintiff's civil rights pleading was 150 pages and described by a federal judge as "inept." Nevertheless, it was held:

> "Where a plaintiff pleads pro-se in a suit for protection of civil rights, the court should endeavor to construe plaintiff's pleading without regard to technicalities."

In *Walter Process Equipment v. Food Machinery*, 382 U.S. 172 (1965) it was held that in a "motion to dismiss, the material allegations of the complaint are taken as admitted." From this vantage point, courts are reluctant to dismiss complaints, unless it appears the plaintiff can prove no set of facts in support of his claim which would entitle him to relief. (see *Conley vs. Gibson*, 355 U.S. 41 (1957).

In *Puckett v. Cox*, it was held that a pro-se complaint requires a less stringent reading than one drafted by a lawyer, (456 F2d 233 (1972 Sixth Circuit USCA) said Justice Black in *Conley v. Gibson*, 355 U.S. 41 at 48 (1957): "The Federal Rules rejects the approach that pleading is a game of skill in which one misstep by counsel may be decisive to the outcome and accept the principle that the purpose of pleading is to facilitate a proper decision on the merits." According to rule 8(f) FRCP, all pleadings shall be construed to do substantial justice."

The Court also cited Rule 8(f) FRCP, which holds that all pleadings shall be construed to do "substantial justice."

It could also be argued that to dismiss a civil rights action or other lawsuit in which a serious factual pattern or allegation of a cause of action has been made, would itself be violative of procedural due process, as it would deprive a pro-se litigant of equal protection of the law vis a vis a party who is represented by counsel.

In a fair system, victory should go to a party who has the better case, not the better representation.

Chapter 19

Prosecutorial Discretion and Selective Prosecution

Prosecutorial Discretion has been defined as the power held by an agency or official charged with enforcement of the law to exercise selectivity in the choice of occasions for the law's enforcement.[1] This essay seeks to focus on cases where such selectivity has been an issue alongside the exercise of the right to freedom of speech and to discuss possible public policies to ensure the evenhandedness of the prosecutorial function. According to the National Advisory Commission on Criminal Justice Standards and Goals, "the decision to charge is one of the least scrutinized discretionary decisions in the administration of justice. The number of persons arrested but not charged with a crime far exceeds the number that are ultimately tried in the courts."[2]

The American Bar Association has decreed that a "prosecutor is not obliged to present all charges which the evidence might support. The prosecutor may in some circumstances and for good cause consistent with the public interest decline to prosecute, not withstanding that evidence may exist which would support a conviction."[3]

Among acceptable criteria for making a decision to charge are:

1. the prosecutor's reasonable doubt that the accused is in fact guilty;
2. the extent of the harm caused by the offense;
3. the disproportion of the authorized punishment in relation to the particular offense or the offender;
4. possible improper motives of a complainant;
5. reluctance of the victim to testify;
6. cooperation of the accused in the apprehending or conviction of others;
7. availability and likelihood of prosecution by another jurisdiction.[4]

Clearly improper motives for bringing prosecutorial action include political considerations, personal advantage or disadvantage or a desire to enhance a record of convictions.[5] In fact, political considerations arise frequently in the exercise of prosecutorial discretion, and the failure of most jurisdictions to take corrective action on such abuses will be shown here as a political, as well as legal, problem.

One of the most important concepts which attorneys seem to agree must rule the prosecutorial function is that "persons similarly situated should be treated the same and criminal justice must be evenly dispensed."[6]

The first major case decided which best embodies this principle is *Yick Wo vs. Hopkins*.[7] In Yick Wo, it was shown that not only the petitioner, but two hundred other persons of Chinese ancestry had applied for a certain business permit, and all were refused. At the same time, all persons of Caucasian ancestry who had applied for the same permit, with one exception, were granted such permits. The Court found that a purposeful and intentional pattern in the application of the permit-granting and penalty statutes existed. The petitioners had been imprisoned for operating their business without a license and were ordered released by the Supreme Court. The discrimination was declared illegal and selective enforcement on a racial basis was held to be a denial of the equal protection of the laws and a violation of the Fourteenth Amendment of the United States Constitution.

Probably no language in Yick Wo has been more quoted than the Court's articulation of the concept of selective prosecution:[(8)]

> Though the law itself be fair on its face and impartial in appearance, yet if it is applied and administered by public authority with an evil eye and an unequal hand, so as practically to make unjust and illegal discriminations between persons in similar circumstances, material to their rights, the denial of equal justice is still within the prohibition of the Constitution.

It would be set forth in a later U.S. Supreme Court case, *Ah Sin v. Wittman*,[(9)] that a burden of proof must be met before a court will seriously consider an allegation of selective prosecution. Alleging selective prosecution alone is insufficient; it must be demonstrated that the "conditions to which the law was directed do no exclusively exist among that class and there are other offenders among that class against whom the law is not enforced"[(10)]

There exist perhaps hundreds of cases in which allegations are made of selective prosecution; only a small minority even attempt to meet the burden of proof described above.

One example of a case in which the burden of proof was met was *United States v. Falk*[(11)] in which the conviction of a defendant who had been charged with refusing to submit to the draft and with failing to possess a registration card was vacated.

Falk was a publicly visible opponent of the selective service system and the Vietnam War. He was able to locate a policy statement of the Selective Service to the effect that the Department of Justice would be asked to prosecute those who publicly burned their draft cards but not those who merely turned their draft cards in. The Court held that it appeared that Falk was indicted and prosecuted for violation of the card possession requirements "only because he exercised his First Amendment privilege to claim a statutory right as a conscientious objector."[(12)]

The court referred to Yick Wo and stated "it is clearly unconstitutional to enable a public official to determine which expression of view will be permitted and which will not or to engage in invidious discrimination among persons or groups... by selective enforcement of an extremely broad prohibitory statute."[(13)]

The court cited *Dixon v. District of Columbia*, 394 F2d 966, 968 (D.C. Cir. 1968) in which Chief Judge Baselon stated:

"The government may not prosecute for the purpose of deterring people from exercising their right to protest official misconduct and petition for redress of grievances. Moreover, a prosecution under such circumstances would be barred by the equal protection clause, since the government employs an impermissible classification..."

The opposition to the draft was not the only protest movement in which allegations of misdirected prosecutorial efforts appeared. During the nineteen sixties, when black citizens of Cairo, Illinois were participating in an economic boycott of merchants alleged to have practiced racial discrimination, it was claimed that the State's Attorney for Alexander County, Illinois, abused his prosecutorial discretion by engaging in selective enforcement and similar misconduct based on a Yick Wo style pattern of discrimination. In Littleton v. Berbling[(14)] it was alleged that:

"Berbling engaged in a pattern of and practice of refusing to allow black citizens to give evidence of criminal conduct committed by white citizens against black citizens. He refuses to initiate criminal proceedings against white citizens arising out of assaults and batteries committed by them against black citizens. He refuses to proceed on black citizens complaints by information or complaint but submits such matters to a grand jury in those instances in which he permits complaints to be filed. He interrogates the black citizens before the grand jury with the purposeful intent of depriving the black citizens of their right to present their evidence to the grand jury. In some instances before the grand jury, he declines to interrogate the black complainants at all.

When white persons are prosecuted on the basis of complaints by plaintiffs, Berbling engages in a practice of inadequately prosecuting in order to lose the cases or to settle them on terms more favorable than those accorded black persons. He engages in a practice of bringing significantly more serious charges against plaintiffs for conduct which would result in no charge or a minor charge against white persons." [(15)]

It was stated that the intent of the defendant was to deprive plaintiffs of the benefits of the criminal justice system and to deter them from "engaging in a peaceful boycott and other activities protected by the First Amendment"[(16)] The United States Court of Appeals (7th Circuit), in Littleton upheld past cases, which decided that an action for damages would not lie against a prosecutor who was performing his duties, no matter what malice was alleged. Plaintiff had sued under 42 U.S.C. § 1981, 1982, 1983 and 1985, seeking in addition to damages, injunctive relief for claims deprivations, under color of law, custom and usage of Cairo, Alexander County, Illinois, of various rights and immunities secured to plaintiffs and members of their class under the Constitution of the United States and the above-named sections of Title 41.[(17)]

The court reiterated what it considers the major reason for prosecutorial immunity:

1. the danger of influencing public officials by threat of a lawsuit;
2. the deterrent effect of potential liability on men who are considering entering public life;

3. the drain on the valuable time of the official caused by insubstantial suits;
4. the unfairness of subjecting officials to liability for the acts of their subordinates;
5. the theory that the official owed a duty to the public and not to the individual;
6. the feeling that the ballot and the Form 1 removal proceeding are more appropriate ways to enforce the honesty and efficiency of public officials."[18]

However, the court did not think that any of the above reasons offered the appropriate means of redressing the grievances alleged by Cairo's black community. Nor did it support the idea of criminal sanctions against public prosecutors.

Instead, the Littleton case advanced the proposal that federal courts may require that periodic reports of various types of aggregate data on actions on bail and sentencing and dispositions of complaints be provided by state courts. The court also quoted favorably a revealing comment about prosecutorial immunity which perhaps tells us more about the court than it does the law:

> The civil damage suit is worthless, especially if the victim of oppression is a social misfit or an unsavory character.[19]

This observer does not know whether the result or reasoning might have been different if movie stars' or politician's children had been involved. The labeling of a person as a "social misfit" tells us absolutely nothing except that the individual was "different;" but perhaps we are beginning to learn a deeper motivation of judicial reasoning. It will be apparent in further cases that the courts are often viewed more as an apparatus of state control and less as a means of redressing injustice when these two interests clash. Thus, selective prosecution is seen, together with other forms of prosecutorial misconduct, as an unfortunate occurrence, but not of sufficient outrage to warrant placing the various states' attorneys at personal financial risk.

However, there remains the use of the defense of selective prosecution when a law, "fair on its face" is being violated by one who can show that its application is unequal.

In 1975, a different kind of case, one with commercial, rather than racial, overtones, emerged in Buffalo, New York. Despite the existence of ordinances which prohibit the opening of certain retailing establishments on Sunday, merchants in many states have committed what might be called an act of civil disobedience. They have remained open on Sundays in order to accommodate their customers who, they say, are being prevented from shopping by a law which violates the separation of church and state guaranteed by the Establishment clause of the First Amendment.

There were many economic reasons for violating the statute also. In *People v. Acme Markets*[20] the New York court was unwilling to declare the church and state issue to be valid, it did reverse a conviction on the basis of selective prosecution. The managers of Acme Markets were able to prove that the local police department had not initiated one single complaint against a violator of a Sunday closing law in thirty-five years. The sole complainant was a local meat-cutter union which did not want its members to have to work on Sundays. So-called "mom and pop" grocery stores, which are less likely to employ meat cutters, were never charged with violating the ordinance.

Enforcement, claimed the petitioners, had been totally surrendered to private parties whom were manipulating the law for purely private purposes. Supermarkets, such as Acme, had been singled out for the enforcement of Sunday closing laws as the city of Buffalo had a policy of prosecuting only on complaints by private citizens. The Courts of Appeals reversed a lower court conviction, holding that discrimination violative of the equal protection clauses of both federal and state constitutions.

Acme Markets illustrates an additional point, critical in debates on a wide variety of criminal justice issues, that an individual police officer's personal sense of justice may lead to his decision to make an arrest. A store which conducts business on Sunday is in plain view of any passing patrolman; how many would actually bother to stop and make an arrest, particularly in view of the spread of violent crime? In all "victimless crimes," particularly narcotics, gambling and prostitution one many reasonably surmise that a great deal of prosecutorial discretion is exercised. Government studies have been focused on the issue and the President's Commission of Law Enforcement and Administration of Justice discovered that:

> "among the types of cases in which thoughtful prosecutors commonly appear disinclined to seek criminal penalties are domestic disturbances; assaults and petty thefts in which victim and offender are in a family or social relationship; statutory rape when both parties are young, teenagers taking a car for a short joy ride; checks that are drawn on insufficient funds; shoplifting by first offenders, particularly when restitution is made; and criminal acts that involve offenders suffering from emotional disorders short of legal insanity."[(21)]

Thus, enforcement of many different laws may be said to be selective; and the possibility might exist that one who is outspoken, one who is a "social misfit" (whatever that means) or one who has antagonized local police or county officials can never really know whether or not he is being charged for the offense itself or for spite. Thus, if an anonymous, unknown housewife bounces a check and a well-known advocate of an unpopular cause does likewise, this kind of problem may well be present.

One kind of prosecution in which the motivation of the decision to charge is rarely obscure are cases of outspoken tax resisters. In the *United States v. Ojala*, [(22)] appellant was convicted of willfully and knowingly failing to make timely filings of his personal tax returns and appealed. The appellant alleged that he was targeted for prosecution because he had exercised his First Amendment rights to protest the Vietnam War, and thus was the victim of unconstitutional selective prosecution.

In dealing with this allegation, the court referred to a two pronged test of "intentional and purposeful discrimination" set forth by the Second Circuit in the *United States v. Berrios*, 501 F.2d 1207, 1211 (2d Cir. 1974):

To support a defense of selective prosecution, a defendant bears the heavy burden of establishment at least prima facie, (1) that, while others similarly situated have not generally been proceeded against because of conduct of the type forming the basis of the charge against him, he has been singled out for prosecution, and (2) that the government's discriminatory selection of him for prosecution has been invidious or in bad faith, i.e., based upon such impermissible considerations as race, religion or the desire to prevent his exercise of constitutional rights... Mere conscious exercise of selectivity in enforcement is not in itself a federal constitutional violation.

The court in Ojala admitted that the defendant made a prima facie showing that he had been selected for prosecution while others similarly situated were not indicted. Ojala had called a press conference on October 30, 1972 in which he stated that he had refused to file returns because of his opposition to the war in Vietnam. Shortly after the press conference, I.R.S. agents started an investigation of the defendant's alleged failure to file his returns.

That the speedy investigation conducted by the government was initiated because the appellant, a well-known politician, announced his purposeful refusal to comply with filing requirements because of his political views, was fully admitted by the I.R.S.

The court stated that this procedure "falls well within the degree of prosecutorial discretion which is historically a part of criminal justice system."(23)

Citing *United States v. Peskin*, 527 F2d 71, 86, (7th Cir. 1975), the court added:

> "It makes good sense to prosecute those who will receive the media's attention. Publication of the proceedings may enhance the deterrent effect of the prosecution and maintain public faith in the precept that public officials are not above the law." (24)

Ojala was upheld in *U.S. v. Catlett*, 584 F.2d 864, (Cir. 1978) which gave the I.R.S. virtually unlimited power to use selective enforcement procedures for the express purpose of deterring the exercise of First Amendment rights by tax protestors.

The defendant was convicted of willfully failing to file an income tax return for three consecutive years and appealed, contending that the I.R.S. pursued criminal prosecution of "nonfilers" who obtained publicity and mainly civil remedies against nonfilers who did not receive publicity.

The court decided that such a pattern of activity did not constitute an abuse of prosecutorial discretion. Its reasoning was as follows:

> "The decision to prosecute, therefore, rests upon the amount of publicity one's protests receive, not upon the exercise of one's First Amendment right to freedom of speech. Such a decision is not based upon an impermissible ground but rather serves a legitimate governmental interest in promoting public compliance with tax laws." (25)

The right of citizens to use the instruments of mass communication for social change has been balanced against public policy requiring voluntary compliance.

The court adopted the reasoning of the Internal Revenue Service which employed a "national public policy" approach:

> We are concerned about the continuing publicity of taxpayers' admitted failures to comply with the Federal tax laws as a means of protest. Our concern is because the publicity of seemingly successful tax violations, regardless of motive, causes of erosion of public confidence in our tax system, with a resultant adverse impact on voluntary compliance.
>
> Much of the "tax protest" publicity in recent years has focused on those protesting American military involvement in Southeast Asia...
>
> Nationally, the Intelligence Division has taken or is taking action against many violators who achieved self-promoted prominence, as tax protestors. We believe the publicity attending these enforcement actions has done much to deter others from embarking on similar courses of illegal action. Our objective is to deter the widespread use of tax noncompliance as a means of protest. We believe a selective approach, rather then a large scale national project, is the most effective and efficient way to achieve this objective. Therefore, primary emphasis will be placed on the identification and investigation of cases in which prosecution will result in the maximum contribution to this objective. These cases will normally be those involving flagrant violations and those involving violations by individuals who have achieved notoriety as tax protestors. Such cases usually provide a vehicle for extensive news coverage which alerts a large segment of the taxpaying public to the consequences of non-compliance. The publicity aspects, of course, require a close working relationship with public information officers.
>
> It is neither our intention nor our desire to suppress dissent or to persecute individuals because they are critical of, the tax system or government policies. Our sole purpose is to further the total service objective of encouraging and achieving the highest possible degree of voluntary (sic) compliance with the tax laws by enforcing statutory sanctions. Therefore, the existing criteria for evaluating information items and selecting cases for criminal investigation must be scrupulously observed, with special emphasis on the high impact cases mentioned above.[26]

Thus, it is maintained that the government interest in encouraging compliance with I.R.S. demands is significantly more favored by the federal courts than whatever First Amendment rights tax protestors may believe were downplayed here. Although the I.R.S. may have had a valid case against Catlett, he might not have been <u>criminally</u> prosecuted had he been a silent protestor. It was I.R.S. distaste for publicity, a political consideration, that prompted the criminal charge.

One of the more difficult tasks in the alleging of selective enforcement is the gathering of evidence as to patterns of discrimination by prosecutors. Jordan v. U.S. Department of Justice, 591 F.2d 753, (D.C. Cir. 1978) has provided some assistance to defendants by holding that law enforcement manuals were not exempt from disclosure under the Freedom of Information Act nor were documents relating to the exercise of prosecutorial discretion by the U.S. Attorney for the District of Columbia exempt as "matters related solely to the internal personnel rules and practices of an agency or as inter-agency or intra-agency memorandums or letters which would not be available by law to a party other than an agency in litigation with the agency."

However, the court in Jordan also held that the privilege of "work product" is applicable to government attorneys. Recipients of bona fide FOIA documents could conceivably learn the many dynamics at work which influence the decision to charge. Studies have been undertaken by social scientists to determine exactly what these dynamics are and the findings would be of interest to those who would prefer selective prosecution and other negative results of prosecutorial discretion. According to a survey done in Seattle:

> The legal system may be viewed as a set of interorganizational exchange, relationships analogous to a ... community game. The participants in the legal system (game) share a common territorial field and collaborate for different and particular ends. They interact on a continuing basis as their responsibilities demand contact with other participants in the process. Thus, the need for the cooperation of other participants can have a bearing on the decision to prosecute. A decision not to prosecute a narcotics offender may be a move to pressure the United States Attorney's office to cooperate on another case. It is obvious that bargaining occurs.(27)

It was also learned that the elite of society are not always treated like others:

> Community leaders may receive special treatment by the prosecutors if they run afoul of the law. A policy of the King County Office requires that cases involving prominent members of the community be referred immediately to the chief criminal deputy and the prosecutor for their disposition. As one deputy noted,
>
> "These cases can be pretty touchy. It's important that the boss knows immediately about this type of case so that he is not caught "flatfooted" when asked about it by the press."(28)

As elected office holders, district attorneys must be responsive to constituents. Constituents, in turn, share a wide variety of individual and social concerns which may come to the attention of district attorneys through any number of sources. For this reason, it may be unlikely to entirely eliminate political considerations from the decision to charge if a given district attorney wishes to be reelected.

The district attorney is also vulnerable politically from infighting with other government agencies. The role of the dissenter in the mind of the prosecutor can be assessed against a background in which there may not be as much prosecutorial discretion as one would think.

Pressure may come from a governor, a labor union (as in Acme Markets), a political association or a commercial enterprise to exercise "discretion" in a given situation. A *guess* ventured here by this observer is that most police departments and administrative agencies generally view dissenters as potentially embarrassing nuisances who may be made an example of if expedient. The prosecutor may be aware of First Amendment rights, but his personal needs may undermine his respect for them. The prosecutor in Littleton might not have been a racist himself but merely have (done) what he thought his constituency would appreciate, however repugnant.

This brings us to the question of what public policy should be to the prosecutor who abuses his discretionary power or to the prosecutor who selectively prosecutes for political reasons (except, perhaps, the I.R.S. which is *allowed* to enforce its Code selectively). The main trend in an overwhelming majority of jurisdictions is to hold the prosecutor immune from a civil suit for damages resulting from their public duties. In addition to Littleton, a leading case with this result is *Ambler v. Pachtman*.(29) Although this was not a First Amendment or selective prosecution case, the holding is pertinent to any lawsuit which seeks to redress a grievance against a prosecutor.

The petitioner in Ambler filed a suit against a state attorney under Title 42 U.S.C. § 1983, alleging that defendant's actions sought to deprive him of constitutional rights. The petitioner in Ambler, who had been convicted of murder, filed a federal habeas corpus petition claiming the respondents had used false testimony and suppressed material evidence at his trial. The petitioner was successful in obtaining his release.

He then brought the § 1983 action against the state attorney, claiming that the latter had knowingly used false evidence and in so doing unlawfully deprived him of his liberties as guaranteed by the constitution.

The bulk of the U.S. Supreme Court's opinion makes a public policy argument for granting absolute immunity under both § 1983 and in common law. The Court held that to deny victims of malicious or dishonest prosecution civil redress was less important than ensuring a "vigorous and fearless performance of the prosecutor's duty."(30)

According to the Ambler decision, the best way to punish corrupt prosecutors is through "professional discipline by an association of his peers" and through application of criminal statutes, which Littleton did not advocate. Neither remedy materially compensates a defendant for the anguish and discomfort he goes through at trial or in jail. He and his family will suffer social ostracization, embarrassment and emotional turmoil. The prosecutor, even if held liable, would probably be covered by liability or malpractice insurance, anyway.

California, like most states, shield its prosecutors from liability and offers the following explanation:

> The office of public prosecutor is one which must be administered with courage and independence. Yet how can this be if the prosecutor is made subject to suit by those accuses and fails to convict? To allow this would open the way for unlimited

> harassment and embarrassment of the most conscientious officials by those who would profit thereby. There would be involved in every case the possible consequences of a failure to obtain a conviction. There would always be a question of possible civil action in case the prosecutor sought to dismiss a case. The apprehension of such consequences would tend toward great uneasiness and toward weakening the fearless and impartial policy which should characterize the administration of this office. The work of the prosecutor would thus be impeded and we would have moved away from the desired objective of stricter and fairer law enforcement.(31)

Also of interest is *Griffith v. Indiana*,(32) in which a local prosecutor was alleged to have added plaintiff's name to a grand jury bill after the latter refused to indict him, with the result that plaintiff was arrested and forced to appear in court repeatedly before the charge was finally **nolle prossed**. The Supreme Court of Indiana, in 1896, dismissed the civil suit, setting a widely cited precedent of prosecutorial immunity.

One of the very few cases in which a prosecutor was held to be liable for damages for maliciously abusing his discretion was *Leong Yau v. Carden*,33 a 1916 Hawaii case. The accused alleged that the county attorney for Honolulu signed and filed a malicious affidavit accusing him of usury. This affidavit was used to procure an arrest warrant and the accused alleged he was deliberately not arrested until nightfall. He further alleged that the prosecutor prevailed upon the sheriff to ask for unreasonably high bail. The prosecutor postponed the case several times and eventually dismissed it.

The prosecution unsuccessfully attempted to rely on the Griffith precedent; but the Hawaii court used a different approach to the issue. Because a local statute held judges liable for misconduct, an extrapolation was made to include prosecutors due to their "quasi-judicial" role:

> A public prosecuting officer, in determining whether certain purported facts which have been brought to his attention justify the accusation and prosecution of a person believed to have committed an offense, acts in quasi-judicial capacity, and he is not to be held liable in damages for an honest mistake or error of judgment in instituting a criminal proceeding... But if he prosecutes without probable cause and with malice he certainly is in no better position than the judge of a court...who proceeds maliciously... private individuals are entitled to the protection of the law against any conduct of such officers which is at once reckless, malicious and damaging.(34)

If prosecutors were to be held liable for charging an accused on the basis of his political activities or First Amendment activities also, the criteria of Leong Yau would be a welcome national policy as opposed to Ambler. One sees a statute on the books to hold persons liable for violating the Constitutional rights of others but is not the exclusion of the persons in the greatest position of temptation to violate the statute defeating of its original purpose?

The courts had a great deal to say about "fearless and courageous" prosecutors but virtually nothing to say about individual rights, the compensation due victims of prosecutorial misconduct or monetary value of a lawsuit for interfering with one's First Amendment rights. The latter should be worth something under § 1983, but the powers that be disagree. Even if one is guilty of a crime but is punished for a proven ulterior motive of the government, this observer believes the criminal justice system has been perverted. The "hidden agenda" of a district attorney or the I.R.S. allows some to go free while others suffer agony. The holding of Yick Wo needs some force to put people in positions of power on notice that they must apply the instruments of justice equally, no matter what their hidden agenda would tell them. Arguments that this would intimidate state attorneys are specious for the very reason that private attorneys run the risk of being sued every time they lose a case for a client; yet they still practice. Why should state employees have it any different? Those who say that it is because the public safety requires it miss the point that suits against prosecutors for malicious prosecution would almost certainly require a showing that no probable cause existed to charge in the first place, something that few prosecutions for a serious crime would lack.

It is agreed that civil suits for the Falk or other First Amendment related cases present an extremely difficult situation involving burdens of proof, probable cause and the determination of prosecutorial motive. Nevertheless, the courts would serve justice better by seeking to adopt such standards. The alternative is to see more holdings of a totalitarian nature, such as Catlett.

Finally, one of the best arguments for making all government officials responsible for their misconduct comes from a dissent of Justice Brandeis' in *U.S. v. Olmstead*:[(35)]

> Decency, security and liberty alike demand that government officials shall be subjected to the rules of conduct that are commands to the citizen. In a government of laws, existence of the government will be imperilled if it fails to observe the law scrupulously. Our government is the potent, omnipresent teacher. For good or for ill, it teaches the whole people by its example. Crime is contagious. If the government becomes a lawbreaker, it breeds contempt for the law; it invites every man to become a law unto himself. It invites anarchy.[36)]

FOOTNOTES

1. R. Joseph: Reviewability of Prosecutorial Discretion, 75 Colum. L. R. 130 (1975)
2. Task Force Report, LEAA, Wash. D.C. (1973)
3. ABA Standards Relating to the Prosecutorial Function
4. id.
5. id.
6. U.S.C.A. Const. Amend. 14 Const. Art. 1 § 11
7. 118 U.S. 356 (1886)
8. 118 U.S. at 373
9. 198 U.S. 500 (1905)
10. id.
11. 479 F.2d 616 (7th Cir. 1973)
12. 479 F.2d at 623
13. id.
14. 468 F.2d at 90 (7th Cir. 1972)

15. id.
16. id.
17. 468 F.2d at 389
18. Note, The Proper Scope of the Civil Rights Act, 66 Harv. L. Rev. 12 85, 1295 n.54 (1953)
19. Breitel: Controls in Criminal Law Enforcement, 27 U. Chi. L. Rev. 427, 434 (1960)
20. 37 NY2d 326, 334 NE2d 555 (1975)
21. The Courts: Task Force Report of President's Commission on Law Enforcement and Administration of Justice, Gov't Printing Office, Wash. D.C. (1967)
22. 540 F.2d 940 (8th Cir. 1976)
23. 540 F.2d at 944
24. id.
25. 584 F.2d at 874
26. 584 F.2d at 831
27. G.F. Cole: The Decision to Prosecute, 4 Law and Society 331 (1970)
28. id.
29. 424 U.S. 409 (1976)
30. id.
31. Pearson v. Reed, 6 Cal. App. 2d 277, 287, 44 P2d. 592, 597 (1935)
32. 146 Ind. 117, 44 NE 1001 (1896)
33. 23 Haw. 362 (1916)
34. 23 Hqw. at 369
35. 277 U.S. 438 (1928)
36. id.

Chapter 20

The Ninth Amendment

The Ninth Amendment to the federal constitution is probably the least understood and therefore is ignored in circumstances where it may be very useful. It reads as follows:

"The enumeration in the Constitution, of certain rights, shall not be construed to deny or disparage others retained by the people."

Estelle Griswold was convicted by the State of Connecticut of violating the state birth control law forbidding the use of contraceptives. In 1965 the Supreme Court of the United States reversed her conviction holding that the Connecticut statute was unconstitutional in that it intruded upon the right of marital privacy in violation of the Ninth Amendment (381 U.S. 474, 85 S.Ct.1678).

Justice William O. Douglas' opinion read in part as follows:

> "In interpreting the Constitution real effect should be given to all the words it uses. Myers U.S. 52, 151, 47 S.Ct 21, 37, 71 I. Ed. 160. The Ninth Amendment to the Constitution may be regarded by some as a recent discovery and may be forgotten by others, but since 1791 it has been a basic part of the Constitution which we are sworn to uphold. To hold that a right so basic and fundamental and so deep rooted in our society as the right of privacy in marriage may be infringed because that right is not guaranteed in so many words by the first eight amendments to the Constitution is to ignore the ninth amendment and to give it no effect whatsoever. Moreover, a judicial construction of this fundamental right is not protected by the Constitution because it is not mentioned in explicit terms by one of the first eight amendments or elsewhere in the Constitution would violate the ninth amendment, which specifically states that the enumeration in the Constitution of certain rights shall not be construed to deny or disparage others retained by the people."

Although one may disagree with the implication that the Supreme Court has done much to protect the citizens of this country from governmental abuses, Justice Douglas was in fact on target about the Ninth Amendment. It is a tremendous resource for lawyers and pro-se litigants who ask to redress grievances for overregulation of our lives and for any abuse of the public by an improper exercise of authority.

The real hurdle is in overcoming certain defenses of both absolute and qualified immunity, as many people experienced in civil rights litigation will tell you.

One of the best treatises published on the Ninth Amendment is available from Barrister's Inn, PO, Box 9411, Boise, Idaho 83707.

To summarize the Barrister's Inn essay very briefly, we can say that the intent of the Ninth Amendment is to give every citizen all rights guaranteed inherently to a person as a free and self-governing individual, especially including all the natural rights of man, which our Creator gave to each and every one of us from the beginning of time and which cannot be surrendered to government. Marital privacy is a prime example of such a right, as would be freedom to travel, the right to procreate, the right of self defense and the right to use one's own power to preserve one's own life or of those in one's family (perhaps freedom of choice in medical treatment can be argued as a Ninth Amendment right), the right to alienate or acquire assets, the right to privacy of one's personal and business matters, i.e. perhaps credit and financial information... and the right to earn a living, among others.

Chapter 21

A Drastic Procedure for Bad State Judges

Title 28 U.S. Code § 1443 permits a defendant in a state court proceeding who is legitimately unsatisfied with the guarantee of equal protection of the law as enforced in the state, to remove the case to federal court. The statute was meant for removal due to racial prejudice. Divorce litigants of the male gender have used it to stop judges in the state domestic relations proceedings from proceeding against them.

Following the instructions in the Local Federal Rules, one can use the federal removal statute to disrupt any state case, if you are the defendant and you act in 30 days after being served.

Nevertheless, the federal courts may in all likelihood send the case back to state court, unless you are claiming discrimination of racial grounds, and persons of male gender or unpopular political affiliation have not been successful in staying in federal court very long. But they prove their point and cause vexation and confusion to their opponent.

I have utilized this maneuver to obtain a satisfactory settlement for a husband who was being legally tortured by a particularly worthless spouse and equally worthless judge.

There is a risk of facing a motion for sanctions, but sometimes brinkmanship pays. I should point out that two female judges in the Divorce Court complained unsuccessfully to the Board of Bar Overseers for my using this tactic.

Habeas Corpus

Both the states' and the federal court system recognize habeas corpus as a fundamental human right. The central issue is always to determine if a habeas corpus writ will issue is whether or not a petitioner is being illegally detained, and if the prisoner should be released.

A prisoner in state custody is authorized to file a writ of habeas corpus directed to a federal court when he alleges that he is in custody "in violation of the Constitution or laws or treaties of the United States." (See 28 U.S.C. § 2254). Prior to filing in federal court, a state prisoner should exhaust his state remedies. Constitutional questions should be litigated throughout the state level before being raised through a federal petition. (See Prisoner Collateral Attacks: Lawyers Co-operative Publishing N.Y. 1991).

Disturbingly, Constitutional scholars, James Liebman and Randy Hertz, (authors of "Federal Habeas Corpus Practice and Procedure" the Michic Co., Charlottesville,VA (1994) write that "In the past two decades, the Supreme Court has erected elaborate procedural obstacles to federal habeas corpus review, sometimes by reversing decisions of the mid-1960's that had widened access to the federal courts and sometimes by layering existing standards with a host of new prerequisites, limitations, and exceptions."

This is not good news for prisoners who do not have funds for lawyers who practice federal criminal appellate law at a "state of the art level."

The erosion of the access to this remedy is an assault on the basic and fundamental human rights on which our democratic society is based.

Fortunately, many federal judges are aware that the procedural pitfalls placed on prisoners are anathema to American concepts of fairness and due process. Liebman and Katz quote Chief Judge Oaks of the 2d Circuit to the effect that the evolution of the law of federal habeas corpus may soon reach the point where more often than not, convictions are immune from federal scrutiny, even where federal constitutional rights have clearly been violated. (See Gonzalez v. Sullivan, 934 F2d. 419 (2d. Cir. 1991)).

Say Liebman and Katz: "Even the slightest miscalculation or inadvertent error in the state or federal courts - by a lawyer or even a prisoner acting pro-se may result in forfeiture of meritorious claims."

Thus a prisoner who proceeds pro-se is at risk, unless she is extremely meticulous claiming the right to seasoned counsel in post-conviction practice is a very obvious necessity.

In many circumstances, public counsel should be available to provide prisoners representation in post-conviction matters. This is not the kind of case to pursue pro-se, due to the high stakes of personal liberty and complexities of the procedure.

There is a presumption that state proceedings are constitutionally and legally correct and federal judges are sometimes reluctant to intervene when they should; thus the necessity of having a highly seasoned practitioner.

Statutory references are as follows:

Title 28 § 2241. **Power to Grant Writ**

(a) Writs of habeas corpus may be granted by the Supreme Court, any justice thereof, the district courts and any circuit judge within their respective jurisdictions. The order of a circuit judge shall be entered in the records of the district court of the district wherein the restraint complained of is had.

(b) The Supreme Court, an justice thereof, and any circuit judge may decline to entertain an application for a writ of habeas corpus and may transfer the application for hearing and determination to the district court having jurisdiction to entertain it.

(c) The writ of habeas corpus shall not extend to a prisoner unless -

(1) He is in custody under or by color of the authority of the United States of is committed for trial before some court thereof; or

(2) He is in custody for an act done or omitted in pursuance of an Act of Congress, or an order, process, judgment or decree of a court or judge of the Untied States; or

(3) He is custody in violation of the Constitution or laws or treaties of the United States; or

(4) He, being a citizen of a foreign state and domiciled therein is in custody for an act done or omitted under any alleged right, title, authority, privilege, protection, or exemption claimed under commission, order or sanction of any foreign state, or under color thereof, the validity and effect of which depend upon the law of nations; or

(5) It is necessary to bring him into court to testify or for trial.

(d) Where an application for a writ of habeas corpus is made by a person in custody under the judgment and sentence of a State court of a State which contains two or more Federal judicial districts, the application may be filed in the district court for the district wherein such person is in custody or in the district court for the district within which the State court was held which convicted and sentenced him and each of such district courts shall have concurrent jurisdiction to entertain the application. The district court for the district wherein such an application is filed in the exercise of its discretion and in furtherance of justice may transfer the application to the other district court for hearing and determination.

§ 2254. State custody; remedies in Federal courts

(a) The Supreme Court, a Justice thereof, a circuit judge, or a district court shall entertain an application for a writ of habeas corpus in behalf of a person in custody pursuant to the judgment of a State court only on the ground that he is in custody in violation of the constitution or laws or treaties of the United States.

(b) An application for a writ of habeas corpus in behalf of a person in custody pursuant to the judgment of a State court shall not be granted unless it appears that the application has exhausted the remedies available in the courts of the State, or that there is either an absence of available State corrective process or the existence of circumstances rendering such process ineffective to protect the rights of the prisoner.

(c) An applicant shall not be deemed to have exhausted the remedies available in the courts of the State, within the meaning of this section, if he has the right under the law of the State to raise, by any available procedure, the question presented.

Mandamus

Since medieval times in England, the writ of mandamus has been an extraordinary problem-solving remedy for aggrieved parties. At the time of the American Revolution, mandamus was already a recognized remedy in the colonies.

At present, both the federal court system and the laws of each individual state recognize the mandamus writ as a remedy.

Professor Chester Antieau's treatise entitled "The Practice of Extraordinary Remedies" (Oceana Publications, N.Y., 1987) contain, perhaps the best explanation of mandamus to be found anywhere.

Professor Antieau defines mandamus as "a common law writ to compel an inferior tribunal, body or person to perform a public duty which duty results from operation of law or from the office, trust or official position of the party to whom the command is directed or to compel the admission of a party to the use and enjoyment of a right or office to which he is entitled and from which he is unlawfully precluded." (See Ariz. Rev. Stats. § 12-2021; California Code of Civil Procedure § 1085).

Antieau traces mandamus to the Magna Carta, and quotes Lord Mansfield to the effect that the writ ought to be used "upon all occasions where the law established no specific remedy, and where in justice and good government there ought to be one."

Thus Antieau concludes that "Mandamus in the United States is an extraordinary legal remedy, a civil action, to compel the performance of public duties."

A defendant in a mandamus action must be under a clear and present duty to perform the act sought to be compelled.

A Mandamus writ may not be issued where an alternative legal remedy is available. (See "The Law of Extraordinary Remedies" Ferris, AMS Press, NY 1926).

According to Professor Antieau, when other litigation between parties is already in progress, it has been possible to initiate the request for a mandamus by motion. This naturally saves the effort of bringing an independent action for the same purpose.

A Federal enabling statute exists for a civil action and a complaint in mandamus; Title 28 U.S. Code § 1361 is entitled "Action To Compel An Officer Of The United States To Perform His Duty." It simply reads:

> The district courts shall have original jurisdiction of any action in the nature of mandamus to compel an officer or employee of the U.S. or any agency thereof to perform a duty owed to the Plaintiff. (Technically, the writ has been abolished, but the cause of action survives in federal court.)

A pro-se litigant can examine the annotated cases in the U.S. Code annotated available in any law library and determine if she/he has a case in which mandamus may be an appropriate remedy, based on previous examples.

Generally, if the relief sought is entirely discretionary with the public servant, mandamus will not be allowed. If it is not, then the claimant may have a chance. (An example of a federal mandamus complaint is attached to this section.)

In many states, stockholders or members of private corporations have the right to use mandamus to enforce their rights as participants in corporate affairs. Generally, however, the remedy is applied to public officials.

Chapter 22

Pleading Conspiracy

The common law in many states will permit you to plead a civil damage count for injuries suffered as a consequence of a conspiracy.

The elements of a civil conspiracy claim include:

1. A combination of persons who (a) plan an unlawful purpose; or (b) utilize an unlawful means.

2. Obtaining a power of "coercion" as a result of the conspiracy from the actions of two or more persons, which would be greater than one person acting alone.

3. Damages.

A count for conspiracy can stand alone or be alleged as a civil tort in connection with another tort (civil wrong) to seek joint liability.

It is absolutely unnecessary to show that a conspirator was aware of the entire scope of the conspiracy, or all of its details, or the identities of its members in order to hold the conspirator liable.

The conspirator can have altogether different motives than other conspirators, can play a very minor role, join the conspiracy late and still be liable both civilly and criminally.

Civil racketeering cases, common law fraud, civil rights cases and cases of tortious conversion are examples where one may use a conspiracy allegation to good advantage.

It has been said that the essence of conspiracy is an "agreement" to do an unlawful act, in which at least one overt act is executed.

A conspiracy may be a continuing one; actors may drop out, and others drop in; the details may change from time to time, the members may not know each other, or the part played by others; a member need not know all the details of the plan or the operations, he must, however, know the purpose of the conspiracy and agree to become a party to a plan to effectuate that purpose. See *Craig v. U.S.*, 81 F2d 816.

In the early days of the American Republic, the common law of conspiracy was being formulated in Massachusetts and survives today. See *Patten v. Gurney*, 17 Mass. 182 (1821) which upheld the proposition that conspirators can be held liable for the damages caused by their conspiracy, even if the planned actions were never completed.

Proving a conspiracy may require extensive use of discovery tools. A deposition in which a defendant is asked to name persons who assisted or who had knowledge of the events which transpired, and what their role was, what their knowledge was and who they spoke to, what the conversations consisted of and similar questions along these lines will be necessary. Interrogatories can also be used.

But using the term "Conspiracy" or "co-conspirator" is loaded. You may use it in your complaint, but asking somebody who their fellow "conspirators" were is too loaded to get answered by anybody who has half a brain. So your discovery questions must be carefully thought out.

Admitting to being part of a conspiracy can lead to jail time, and the facts gathered in a civil suit can at least theoretically be used in a criminal case. In other words, be discreet in how you phrase interrogatories.

In criminal cases, conspiracy charges make the sentence longer, much longer.

They can be used by a prosecutor to force somebody to accept a relatively lighter sentence by pleading guilty, even when there is a defendable case, to avoid the risk of a 20 year visit to one of our government's finer facilities by facing a weak conspiracy allegation where the "justice system" might not work too well, and the government prevails.

Two or more acts in furtherance of a conspiracy to obstruct justice are sufficient to make a Racketeering case, if you can also allege that there was some kind of connection to a "legitimate business." See Title 18 U.S. Code 1964, et. seq.

Chapter 23

Summary of the Fair Debt Collection Practices Act

Not many people enjoy being contacted by debt collectors, but, let's face it, it's probably impossible to go through life without it.

Congress is aware of the impact collection agencies have on consumers, and also the abuses that occur when the agencies are not controlled.

For this reason Congress passed Title 15 USC Section 1601, The Fair Debt Collection Practices Act, which establishes limits on the behavior of debt collectors and collection agencies towards consumers.

Unfair or unconscionable methods of collecting a debt are prohibited by the Act. These methods include, but are not limited to, the following:

1. Using or threatening to use violence to injure any person or property.

2. The use of obscene language.

3. Annoying or frequent telephone calls. Making telephone calls before 8:00 a.m. or after 9:00 p.m.

4. Threatening criminal prosecution (except when a bad check is involved.)

5. Falsely implying that the collector is a lawyer.

6. Communicating the existence of the debt to a third party without permission of the debtor.

7. Communicating with the debtor when the debtor has retained a lawyer.

8. Using post cards to communicate with a debtor.

9. Soliciting a post dated check from a debtor and then threatening to deposit it to precipitate a criminal prosecution.

The law provides remedies, including the right to file a class action lawsuit for up to $500,000.

Under certain circumstances, collection agencies may also be sued for intentional infliction of emotional anguish and even under the Federal racketeering statute, if the threat of violence or a pattern of fraudulent activity using the mail is occurring.

Chapter 24

Federal Claims After State Litigation

All too often, a victim of a civil rights violation gets no justice in the State court system and wishes to somehow have an opportunity to have the merits of the case heard before a federal judge.

More often than not, the state forum was probably part of the problem.

It may have been that the state court was biased, that one lawyer was friendly with the clerk or the judge and that you never had a meaningful hearing before the state system.

It may have been that constitutional issues were never decided in the state forum, even though other aspects of the case were.

There may have been institutional or political biases against you or your lawyer, or perhaps the lawyer was inarticulate or unprepared.

In any event, you were shafted in state court, somewhere along the lines, your constitutional rights were violated, and now you want to make a federal case.

Many cases have followed the path of Rooker v. Fidelity Trust, 263 U.S. 413 (1923) which has been interpreted as "foreclosing federal suit on any section 1983 claim which could have been raised in a previous state action." This references Title 42 USC § 1983, a federal civil rights statute.

All kinds of fancy defenses, such as res judicata (the thing has already been decided), collateral estoppel and the doctrine of issue preclusion are going to be raised in federal court to send you home.

Wayne McCormack's text entitled *Federal Courts* (Matthew Bender, NY 1984) contains some valuable insight on the ways to circumvent these defenses. It is difficult, but not impossible.

An important part of the strategy may be to claim that the state court judgment was somehow "constitutionally infirm," and hence need not be given full recognition by the federal court.

McCormack mentions that: It has been suggested that relitigation should take place whenever one or more of the following factors is present to a degree that preclusion would be likely to compromise the federal court's own role in articulating and implementing constitutional principles;

1. The state court or agency had an institutional interest in deciding as it did.

2. The constitutional claim refers to the manner of the state decision rather than to the point of original dispute between the parties.

3. The issue relates more to a person's relationship with the state than with another person.

4. The state decision was made without a full and fair hearing of the facts.

5. There is a special need for federal court fact finding.

6. The plaintiff initially had or reasonably believed that he had no choice of forum.

7. The remedies sought in federal court differ significantly from those available in state proceedings.

Naturally, you want to characterize your federal lawsuit as an action based in as many of these situations as you arguably can.

The dissenting opinion in *Brown v. Chastain*, 416 F2d 1012 (5th Cir. 1969) clearly indicates that some options are available if you have the right facts in your case.

The dissent in *Brown* argued that rather than the issue of relitigating the same facts twice, more importantly a solicitous regard for fundamental rights made cases in which constitutional claims were being asserted likely exceptions to res judicata.

Unfortunately, this is a minority view. See also *Tribune Review Publishing Co. V. Thomas*, 150 F. Supp. 362.

Chapter 25

Fair Credit Reporting Act Can Protect Your Reputation

The Fair Credit Reporting Act, Title 15 U.S. § 1681 is a federal law intended to insure "fairness, impartiality and a respect for a consumer's right to privacy" in relation to consumer reporting agencies which advise banks, credit card issuers and all other credit grantors as to a consumer's credit worthiness.

The Act establishes a procedure for correcting mistakes on your credit record. Whenever a consumer has good reason to believe that a report about his or her credit or any other information on the report (sometimes including character and drinking habits) is not accurate, it is the responsibility of the consumer to contact the reporting agency and to explain the situation.

The consumer reporting agency must, within a reasonable time, review the information and conduct an investigation, unless, says the statute, they believe the consumer's dispute is "frivolous or irrelevant."

Consumer reporting agencies must otherwise correct the file, if after an investigation, good reason would seem to exist. If there is still a dispute, a consumer must file a brief statement giving his side of the story, which must be included in all future credit reports. Such a report may be as long as 100 words.

Whenever credit is denied on the basis of a report by a consumer reporting agency, a consumer must be notified and given the name and address of the reporting agency. The agency must supply the consumer with a copy of his or her credit report.

In the event a bank, credit card company or other source supplies a consumer credit reporting service with erroneous information, that source may be sued by an aggrieved consumer for negligence.

The Fair Credit Reporting Act provides many causes of both criminal and civil action for violations.

Any person who obtains information on a consumer from a consumer reporting agency under a false pretense can be subjected to substantial criminal penalties, as well as sued for any damages caused thereby.

If an officer or employee of a consumer reporting agency provides consumer data to an unauthorized party, this is also grounds for both civil and criminal liability.

A 1976 case in Michigan brought in federal court *(Collins v. Retail Credit Co.)* resulted in a $321,500 jury verdict for a consumer who sued a consumer reporting agency for libel and violations of the Fair Credit Reporting Act.

The Retail Credit Company was found to have prepared an untrue investigative report of the consumer, using careless research methods and maintaining a reckless disregard of the truth. Additionally, the company was found to have breached its statutory obligation to reinvestigate and delete information disputed by a consumer when good reason existed to do so.

Many, if not all, states also regulate consumer reporting agencies. Lawsuits brought in a federal court under the Fair Credit Reporting Act may also include additional claims for violations of state laws.

Truth In Lending

Enacted by the Administration of Lyndon Johnson in 1968, the Truth In Lending Act was designed for the purpose of encouraging "informed use of credit." In the introduction to the Act it states:

"The informed use of credit results from an awareness of the costs thereof by consumers. It is the purpose of this title to assure a meaningful disclosure of credit terms so that the consumer will be able to compare more readily the various credit terms available to him, and avoid the uninformed use of credit, and to protect the consumer against inaccurate and unfair credit billing and credit card practices."

Responsibility for implementing the Act lies with the Federal Trade Commission and the Board of Governors of the Federal Reserve System. The law requires the disclosure of the actual finance charge in each and every consumer credit transaction and outlines specific instructions for calculating the finance charge.

Lenders must calculate not only interest, but also any amount payable under a point, discount or other additional charges. They must include the service or carrying charges, loan fees, finder's fees, fees for an investigation or credit report and the time/price differential, which discloses the higher interest rates which apply when a loan is stretched out for a longer period of time. Lenders must also include in their calculation of the finance charge the cost of any insurance or other guarantee against default or other credit loss.

In a consumer credit transaction which includes a lien on his or her home, a homeowner is allowed by the statute to rescind such an agreement within 72 hours.

This applies most frequently to second mortgage situations or home improvement contracts, but not to first mortgages.

A consumer defrauded in such a transaction or who has suffered damages by a violation of the Trust In Lending Act may bring a lawsuit in the United States District Court for not only his or her actual loss, but also twice the amount of the total finance charge.

Businesses which violate the Truth In Lending Act may be sued for $500,000.00 or more, depending on the circumstances, by means of a class action i.e. multiple plaintiffs joining together in one lawsuit, if a pattern of violations exists. They may also face criminal penalties of $5,000.00 in fines and a one year jail term for each offense.

Chapter 26

Attachments, Garnishments and Liens

This author defines attachments as "recorded contingent interests in real property derived from litigation." After all, there will be a permanent seizure of the attached real estate if the lawsuit is successful.

The result of the lawsuit, of course, is the contingency of which we speak.

How does one obtain a real estate attachment?

According to the Federal Rules of Civil Procedure, the methods of freezing assets in a federal suit are based on state law. In Massachusetts, then, we would look to the Massachusetts Rules of Civil Procedure and the rules governing attachments.

Judges allow attachments by motion. A party files a Motion For Real Estate Attachment together with an Affidavit giving the following basis:

1. A substantial likelihood of recovery.

2. The absence of any insurance coverage to satisfy a judgment.

3. The lack of good faith defenses which can be raised by the Defendant.

4. Give some history of the circumstances of the case which give rise to your claim, the damages or injuries suffered.

5. State the sum you wish to attach the property for.

Although the property of bureaucracies such as the FBI or other state or federal agencies is exempt from attachment, the property of individual bureaucrats is not.

Ex parte attachments are available in some circumstances on an emergency basis, especially of bank accounts.

"Ex parte" means without a party, that party being the defendants.

The constitutionality of ex parte attachments and even pre-trial attachments has come under wide attack.

The liability of lawyers who attach property without giving notice of a hearing to the defendant is worth considering under Title 42 U.S. Code § 1983, as this is essentially a violation of procedural due process.

If you do attach property, you are required to deliver the attachment writ to the local sheriff and the sheriff will record it at the local registry of deeds.

Common law liens are not court ordered. They arise when a skilled tradesman holds on to the goods he takes care of. Automobile or boat mechanics, for example, need not release the vehicles they work on until they have been paid.

Some persons will try to cloud titles by filing liens against defendants without court approval. Some registries apparently allow any document to be filed. Persons who try to use Deed Registries to file common law liens risk lawsuits themselves for defamation of title, abuse of process and similar causes of action.

Chapter 27

Claims For False Arrest and False Imprisonment

False imprisonment is a claim that can be made under state law. It is considered a "tort," that is a claim made for a personal injury. A false imprisonment claim generally includes the unlawful arrest or detention of a person without a warrant, or by a falsely issued warrant, in a prison or other confinement, or seizure by force and constraint without confinement, but with the deprivation of personal liberty. See *Jordan v. Pike*, 302 Mass. 281 (1939).

The elements of a false imprisonment claim include:

1. An unlawful restraint upon the victim's freedom by the imposition of force and threats.

2. Damages.

If the underlying arrest is legal, the claim for false imprisonment is weak. If the underlying arrest is unlawful, the claim for false imprisonment is strong.

Thus the defenses of justification, for example, a valid citizen's arrest is a likely defense to a claim for false imprisonment. A criminal conviction, which has not be successfully challenged, is a likely defense also.

A false arrest is another constitutional tort cognizable under common law of the states.

The standard for a false arrest is "reasonable grounds." The fourth amendment to the federal constitution protects us from "unreasonable search and seizure," which is in fact a reference to "arrest," being a seizure of a person.

When government has participated in the false arrest or false imprisonment, redress is available through federal civil rights actions. However, if a private party has violated your rights, the common law remedy in state court may well be your most practical means of redress.

Chapter 28

Claims Against The IRS
Excerpts From An IRS Legal Brief

Under certain circumstances, an individual may bring a claim against an officer or employee of the United States to recover damages for infringement of certain constitutional rights by the federal officer or employee. *Bivens v.. Six Unknown Named Agents of the Federal Bureau of Narcotics*, 403 U.S. 388, 396-97 (1971); *G.M. Leasing Corp. v. United States*, 429 U.S. 338, 360 (1977). Courts, however, have specifically declined to hold that a plaintiff may bring a Bivens action when the alleged deprivation of rights occurred during the collection of federal taxes.

McMillen v. U.S. Dept. Of Treasury, 960 F.2d 187, 190 (1st Cir. 1991) (citing *Cameron v. IRS*, 773 F.2d 126, 129 (7th Cir. 1985)) (Court doubtful that creation of a Bivens remedy is an appropriate response to violations by IRS, given exclusive remedies in §§ 7432 and 7433.) See also *Baddour, Inc. v. United States*, 802 F.2d. 801, 807-809 (5th Cir. 1986). The rationale for not allowing Bivens actions in cases involving internal revenue taxes is that Congress has already created explicit remedies to protect taxpayers in their disputes with the Internal Revenue Service, and a court-created remedy would interfere with the effective functioning of government. *Cameron v. IRS*, 773 F.2d 126, 129 (7th Cir. 1985); see also *American Assn. of Commodity Traders v. Department of Treasury*, 598 F.2d 1233, n.2 (1st Cir. 1979) ("Judicial remedies are implied from the constitution only when there is no direct means for redress already available.")

The Supreme Court underscored this point in its decision in *Schweiker v. Chilicky*, 487 U.S. 412 (1988), which was a suit for damages for the unwarranted deprivation of Social Security benefits. The injuries in that case-deprivation of money needed for food, shelter, and medicine-were without redress under the administrative process for review and adjudication of disputed claims. Despite the fact that a serious injustice, which had deprived plaintiff of the very necessities of life, would go unremedied, the Court, relying on its decisions in *Bush v. Lucas*, 462 U.S. 367 (1983), and Bivens itself, rejected the plaintiff's contention that a Bivens remedy should be created to provide relief for injuries that could not be fully redressed by the Social Security Act. Even assuming a constitutional violation, the Court stated that "[t]he absence of statutory relief for a constitutional violation... does not by any means necessarily imply that courts should award money damages against the officers responsible for the violation." Chilicky, 487 U.S. at 421-22.

The Supreme Court cautioned that, in an area governed by a carefully designed framework of statutory remedies, Congress is in a better position than the courts to decide whether the creation of a damage remedy for "constitutional torts" would serve the public interest. The Chilicky case made it clear that it was the comprehensiveness of the statutory scheme involved, not the adequacy of the specific remedies thereunder, that counseled judicial abstention. *Spagnola v. Mathis*, 859 F.2d 223, 227 (D.C. Cir. 1988). The Internal Revenue Code is an example of such a comprehensive statutory scheme.

Federal taxation is an area involving policy questions that have received careful attention from Congress. As a result of these Congressional deliberations, the Internal Revenue Code strikes a balance between the protection of citizens allegedly aggrieved by agency action and the protection of the individuals enforcing the revenue laws. The Code provides for an elaborate system whereby taxpayers are afforded remedies for agency errors or misconduct. Taxpayers may seek refunds of taxes paid upon allegations that the amounts paid or collected were excessive and they may, before payment, contest proposed deficiencies in income, estate, or gift taxes. 26 U.S.C. §§ 7422, 6213. Non-taxpayers have the right to sue when their property is wrongfully levied upon. 26 U.S.C. § 7426. A taxpayer may sue for damages for the unauthorized disclosure of return information. 26 U.S.C. § 7431.

Since 1988, amendments to the Internal Revenue Code, informally known as the Taxpayer Bill of Rights, added to the means available to taxpayers to redress alleged agency misconduct. Taxpayers can sue for civil damages against the United States, if an Internal Revenue Service employee fails, under certain circumstances, to release a lien on the taxpayers's property. 26 U.S.C. § 7432. And, as is the case in this action, taxpayers can sue for damages which allegedly result from an Internal Revenue Service employee's alleged reckless or intentional disregard of the Internal Revenue Code or Treasury regulations during the collection process. 26 U.S.C. § 7433. Nowhere in this elaborate scheme has Congress established a personal damages remedy for statutory or constitutional violations.

Furthermore, Congress expressly provided that section 7433 be the exclusive remedy for recovering damages resulting from the intentional or reckless disregard of the Internal Revenue Code and its regulations in connection with the collection of federal taxes.[2] :26 U.S.C. § 7433(a). Deference to that legislative judgment in fashioning exclusive federal remedies is required by "the Court's longstanding recognition that Congress is ultimately the appropriate body to create federal remedies." *Carlson v. Green*, 446 U.S. 14, 27 (1980) (Powell, J., concurring in the judgment); see also McMillen, 960 F.2d at 190-91 (1st Cir. 1991), Baddour, Inc., 802 F.2d at 129 (7th Cir. 1985).

The tax area is replete with restrictions designed to limit carefully the judicial review of tax disputes with the United States and, especially, to shield individual employees from personal liability. The Federal Tort Claims Act, for example, excepts actions involving the collection and assessment of taxes. 28 U.S.C.§ 2680(c).[3] Where an individual is named in a refund suit or a wrongful levy action, the code requires that the United States be substituted as the defendant. 26 U.S.C. §§ 7422(f), 7426(c). The Taxpayer Bill of Rights are limited to actions against the United States, even though an individual's misconduct creates the cause of action. 26 U.S.C. §§ 7432(a), 7433(a). The constant theme in the tax area is that individual officials charged with enforcement of internal revenue laws should be shielded from personal liability. Source: Defendant's Brief Barron v. Greeley, et al, U.S. District Court, NH; Docket No. C-97-271-JD

Chapter 29

Rule 60

When a court decides against you in a civil trial, you have other options besides or in addition to the appeal process. According to the Federal Rules of Civil Procedure, Rule 60, several grounds exist for the vacation of a judgement:

Rule 60, Relief From Judgment or Order

(A) Clerical Mistakes. Clerical Mistakes in judgements, orders or other parts of the record and errors therein arising from oversight or omission may be corrected by the court at any time of its own initiative or on the motion of any party and after such notice, if any, as the court order. During the pendency of an appeal, such mistakes may be so corrected before the appeal is docketed in the appellate court, and thereafter while the appeal is pending may be so corrected with the leave of the appellate court.

(B) Mistakes, Inadvertence; Excusable Neglect; Newly Discovered Evidence; Fraud, Etc. On motion and upon such terms as are just, the court may relieve a party or his legal representative from a final judgment, order, or proceeding for the following reasons; (1) mistake, inadvertence, surprise, or excusable neglect; (2) newly discovered evidence which by due diligence could not have been discovered in time to move for a new trial under Rule 59(b); (3) fraud (whether heretofore dominated intrinsic or extrinsic, misrepresentation, or other misconduct of an adverse party; (4) the judgment is void; (5) the judgment has been satisfied, released, or discharged, or a prior judgment, upon which it is based has been reversed or otherwise vacated, or it is no longer equitable that the judgment should have prospective application; or (6) or any other reason justifying relief from the operation of the judgment. The motion shall be made within a reasonable time, and for reasons (1), (2), and (3) not more than one year after the judgment, order or proceeding was entered or taken. A motion under this subdivision (b) does not affect the finality of a judgment or suspend its operation. This rule does not limit the power of the court to entertain an independent action to relieve a party from a judgment, order, or proceeding, or to grant relief to a defendant not actually personally notified as provided in Title 28, U.S.C., § 1655, or to set aside a judgment for fraud upon the court. Writs of coram nobis, coram vobis, audita querela, and bills of review and bills in the nature of a bill of review are abolished, and the procedure for obtaining any relief from a judgment shall be by motion as prescribed in these rules or by an independent action.

Of particular interests in this chapter is the use of Rule 60(B)(6) when things don't go your way.

Rule 60(B)(6) has been described as the "catch-all" clause. *Menier v. United States*, (5th Cir. 1968), 405 F.2d 245, 248 because it provided the court with a "grand reservoir of equitable power to do justice in a particular case" 7 Moore, s60.27(2) at 375, *Radack v. Norwegian American Line Agency, Inc.*, (2d Cir. 1963), courts adequate to enable them to vacate judgments whenever such action is appropriate to accomplish justice," *Klapprott v. United States*, 335 U.S.

at 615, 69S Ct. At 390 where relief might not be available under any other clause in 60(b), *Transit Casualty Company v. Security Trust Company*, (5th Cir. 1971), 441 F.2d 788, 792, Cert. denied, 404 U.S. 883, 92 S.Ct. 211, 30 L.Ed.2d 164.

Federal Rules of Civil Procedure Rule 60(B)(6) allows the district court to vacate an order for any reason justifying relief provided the party seeking files such a motion within a reasonable time and provided the reasons for such relief are not governed by the first five subdivisions of the rule. Fed.R.Civ.P. 60(B)(6); see *Liljeberg v. Health Services Acquisition Corp.,* 486 U.S. 747, 863, 108 S.Ct.2194, 2204, 100 L.Ed.2d 855 (1988).

A motion for relief under Rule 60(B) is addressed to the sound discretion of the court. *Neimaizer v. Baker,* 793 F.2d 58, 61 (2d Cir.1986). The court must weigh the interest in substantial justice against the need for preserving finality of judgments. Id. Therefore, relief is granted only for extraordinary circumstances. *Mendell v. Gollust*, 909 F.2d 724, 730 (2d Cir. 1990) aff'd--- U.S.---, 111 S.Ct.2173, 115 L.Ed.2d 109 (1991).

This rule vests power in the courts adequate to enable them to vacate judgments whenever such action is appropriate to accomplish justice. E*xpenditures Unlimited Aquatic Enterprises, Inc.v. Smithsonian Institute*, 1974, 500 F.2d. 808, 163 U.S. App.D.C. 140. See also, *Brown v. Clark Equipment Co.,* D.C. Mc. 1982, 961 F.R.D. 166.

The desire of the courts to repair injustice wrought by judgment will overcome necessity for finality of judgment where it is against conscience to execute the judgment and where judgment was rendered without fault or neglect on part of party seeking to reform it. *West Virginia Oil & Gas Co. v. George Breece Lumber Co.,* C.A. 5(La.)1954, 213 F.2d. 702.

CHAPTER 30

Sue the System for Racketeering

A number of precedents seem to indicate that it is possible to bring civil RICO lawsuits against political appointees, judges, courthouses and bureaucracies and bureaucrats, who would ordinarily be otherwise immune.

RICO refers to the Racketeer Influenced Corrupt Organizations Act, Title 18 U.S. Code, Sect 1961 which is a statute with criminal and civil provisions for suing business organizations and individuals who use the proceeds of criminal activity to further a "legitimate enterprise" or infiltration of a legitimate enterprise.

Robert Bacheler and Rocco Cipparone were employees of the Philadelphia Traffic Court back in the nineteen seventies. They were investigated and convicted of engaging in a racketeering conspiracy and of filing false tax returns.

Among the conclusions of the federal trial court was a finding that the Philadelphia Traffic Court was an "enterprise" within the meaning of the Racketeering Influenced Corrupt Organizations Act, Title 18 U.S.C. Sect. 1961. The defendants, court employees were both taking bribes and forgetting to declare them as income.

On appeal they argued that a Court could not be a racketeering enterprise for the purposes of the RICO act but were not successful. Their precedent is one which subjects every dishonest courthouse employee to a civil suit as well, and these suits include the ability to claim triple damages.

Pennsylvania federal judge Sloviter, a Third Circuit US Court of Appeals Judge made the decision in *U.S. v. Bacheler*, 611 F.2d 443.

One shouldn't doubt for a minute that if the case was a civil lawsuit by a pro-se litigant against a crooked courthouse employee that the judicial reasoning might not have been the same. But the *Bacheler* case was a criminal prosecution (RICO has both criminal and civil components) and this criminal case should pave the way for future cases. Racketeering includes obstruction of justice, and other kinds of criminal acts that occasionally turn up in courthouses.

State court magistrates have also been convicted under RICO laws. Magistrates in Allegheny Pennsylvania were accused of conspiracy to accept bribes offered by bail bondsmen for lucrative referrals. The FBI investigated and the case was ultimately prosecuted in federal court in Pittsburgh. See *U.S. vs. Herman*, 589 F.2d 1191.

If they are criminally liable under the law, the same law should not immunize them from civil suits under the statute.

As a practical matter RICO lawsuits against courthouse employees, politicians and soon will most likely be brought by pro-se litigants. How many lawyers would open themselves up to the harassment that they would certainly receive?

But federal prosecutors have less fears than other lawyers. The Pennsylvania Bureau of Cigarette and Beverage Taxes was also declared a "racketeering enterprise." See *U.S. v. Frumento,* 563 F.2d 1063.

A crooked cabal of tobacco tax officials, cigarette wholesalers and political hacks decided to conspire to smuggle cigarettes into the Commonwealth of Pennsylvania using counterfeit tax stamps. They were criminally prosecuted under RICO; there should be no reason why the civil provisions of the law cannot be applied to them and other corrupt officials who cause harm to the individuals.

Test cases may eventually wind up in the U.S. Supreme Court, but I venture to predict that the bureaucrats will wind up being civilly liable to the public under RICO.

Practical advice to pro-se litigants: Check the American Jurisprudence Pleadings and Forms or similar volumes before filing a civil RICO suit. They are highly complex and minuscule errors can result in dismissal. It is important to allege the defendants engaged in two criminal acts, i.e. bribery or obstruction of justice or other offenses enumerated in the statute and that the plaintiff was harmed by these acts. It is also necessary to allege that the defendants were infiltrating a legitimate business enterprise of some kind and using the criminal activity in some manner to further a legitimate business endeavor.

Read the annotations in United States Code Annotated under Title 18 Section 1962 and 1964.

It is necessary to have a thorough understanding of both the law and the pleading requirements before undertaking litigation in this field.

Chapter 31

How to Harness the Power of a Small Claims Action

Never underestimate the power of a small claims case.

While small claims rules vary from state to state, our research indicates that most states have similar rules and procedures for small claims actions.

Many people leave small claims frustrated even ***after winning*** about what they see as the ineffective nature of the procedure, especially because they have problems recovering on their judgment.

Small claims can be effective, if you know what the rules are and how to implement them. Every small claims session has procedural rules. Do not go to small claims court or even initiate a case unless you have read the rules and understand them.

Small claims courts are usually near you, and are designed to help people resolve cases without a lawyer, when the damages are limited. In Massachusetts, the limit is $2,000.00.

Rules of evidence are relaxed, and in Massachusetts there is no discovery, although witnesses may be subpoenaed.

Small claims cases are not decided by judges any longer in Massachusetts. Clerks have been assigned the role of judges and general principles of jurisprudence and common law have great weight in these sessions.

Trials are held. If lawyers appear, the procedure might be a bit more formal and intimidating for a pro-se litigant.

Clerk's offices will help you obtain the procedural rules. From time to time, various advocacy groups distribute manuals on how to use the small claims system.

Generally, you should have as much paperwork as possible to support your claim.

Write out in a well organized fashion the arguments you wish to make. Make your argument and refer to documents to place into evidence. Bring one copy of each document for your opponent and one for the court, which will impress the judge (or clerk).

Have a constable or other process server subpoena witnesses. This will compel their attendance at trial.

If payment of a bill is in issue, bring cancelled checks or a receipt or expect to lose.

A few tips:

1. Find out the legal business name of a company. If they are a corporation, they should be named exactly as they appear on their official corporate papers, as filed with the state's corporations office. Trusts are sued as "John Jones, Trustee, ABC Realty Trust." Naming a party inaccurately causes problems down the road. It may make your judgment unenforceable. Partners are sued as individuals, and every partner in a partnership can be named.

2. If you are suing an individual, find out at the Registry of Deeds if the individual owned property in his or her name.

3. If you win, determine if you would rather seize the real estate or ask the court to place the defendant on a payment schedule. Many states will issue an Execution which can be used to seize and auction real estate. The Execution can be used to seize real estate or business assets.

   The small claims court clerk will only issue an Execution if you request it.

The Execution is a writ designed to allow you to command a sheriff to seize assets to satisfy a judgment.

If assets cannot be located, you must take the path of what is called "supplementary process."

A supplementary process case is brought when you have a judgment and the defendant will not honor it.

The defendant is sued a second time and this is a suit for the purpose of finding out what the debtor has, what he owes, what he can afford to pay and getting a court order to make him pay.

The defendant's records can be subpoenaed, as can witnesses and custodians of records.

When a defendant fails to obey a court order for payment, he is in contempt, and can be punished.

When a defendant fails to appear for a supplementary process hearing, a civil warrant for his arrest, known as a capias, can be issued.

A constable or sheriff has the power to jail a contemptuous debtor with a capias.

Knowing these pieces of information before you go to small claims court will make you more effective once you get there.

Typical small claims situations are the ruined suit at the drycleaner's (a case of negligence), a credit line at the hardware store gone bad (goods sold and delivered), or the root canal unpaid for (professional services rendered.) However, any kind of action not "pre-empted" by statutes requiring filing elsewhere can be a small claim action.

After a small claims experience, a pro-se litigant may be more comfortable in a more complex legal situation.

Chapter 32

How to Recognize Legal Malpractice and What to Do If it Happens to You

With the explosion of litigation in our society and the abundance of lawyers, more and more people are finding themselves involved in lawsuits. Getting involved with lawyers is not much fun. It can be extremely expensive and draining emotionally as well.

Moreover, a lawyer who does not perform in a professional manner can seriously injure the financial and other rights of his clients. Legal malpractice is a national epidemic, as has been recognized by former Chief Justice Warren Burger who has been quoted as saying that 75% of all lawyers are "dishonest or incompetent." While undoubtedly an exaggeration, this remark was no doubt based on some upsetting observations.

Before you hire a lawyer, please do one thing.

Ask your lawyer if he carries malpractice insurance, and to show you a copy of the policy.

If he doesn't or if he is perturbed that you ask the question, don't hire him. Why?

Because if there is no insurance to cover his mistakes, you may never get justice if your lawyer makes a mistake, and the chances are not unreasonable that he (or she) will.

There are five common mistakes that lawyers make, and here is how they affect you.

1. Lawyers often forget to keep calendars up to date, and miss important deadlines for filing documents. It could mean forgetting to file pleadings in litigation, or even forgetting to appear in a court hearing. It happens more often than you would care to imagine.

2. Lawyers often forget to send important documents or copies of pleadings to clients. This can interfere with how a case is handled and its eventual outcome.

3. Lawyers can get pressured for cash and settle cases too low. Massachusetts courts now permit lawyers to be sued for settling cases too low.

4. Lawyers often do not listen to clients. Too many lawyers do not respect the client enough to listen to the client, return phone calls, and to allow the client sufficient input into handling of the case. Guess who ends up paying in the end?

5. Poor preparation. Too many lawyers are lax when it comes to the handling of trial preparation. Failure to interview witnesses, failure to rehearse favorable witnesses before putting them on the stand, and poor investigations hamstring the lawyer at trial, or force a low settlement. Moreover, thorough legal research is often required, but not done.

A major factor which leads to this problem is that lawyers, often pressed for money, will practice outside their field. The American Bar Association recognizes 49 areas of specialty.

A lawyer cannot possibly keep up with the changes in the law in more than 2 or 3 areas.

So what do you do?

Make sure your lawyer specializes. Don't let a lawyer who is an expert in trusts handle a criminal defense trial unless he is really qualified.

Ask your lawyer what his expertise is.

Understand what kind of relationship you will have with your lawyer before it gets going, to help prevent a malpractice situation from arising.

Have a fee agreement in writing. Tell your lawyer you want to be kept informed of all developments in the case, and receive copies of all documents and pleadings.

Let the lawyer know that returning phone calls is important, and drop notes to the lawyer to keep a paper trail to memorialize what you are trying to tell him. Naturally, keep copies of the letters and notes you send the lawyer.

If things work out badly, ask for your file. Go to the courthouse and make a copy of what the official file contains.

If you notice some troubling issues, such as a case being dismissed for something your lawyer didn't do, such as appear for a motion or filing a pleading, you must locate a lawyer who is willing to sue other lawyers.

There aren't a whole lot of such lawyers.

Thus it is important to learn how to do it yourself if you want justice.

Appendices

Appendix A **Civil Rights Complaint** - Paula Corbin Jones v. William Jefferson Clinton

[A]

IN THE UNITED STATES DISTRICT COURT
FOR THE EASTERN DISTRICT OF ARKANSAS
WESTERN DIVISION

PAULA CORBIN JONES	:	
Plaintiff,	:	CIVIL ACTION
	:	NO. LR-C- 94 - 290
v.	:	
WILLIAM JEFFERSON CLINTON	:	JURY TRIAL DEMANDED
and	:	
DANNY FERGUSON	:	This case assigned to District Judge Wright
Defendants.	:	and to Magistrate Judge Forster

COMPLAINT

Plaintiff Paula Corbin Jones, by counsel, brings this action to obtain redress for the deprivation and conspiracy to deprive Plaintiff of her federally protected rights as hereafter alleged, and for intentional infliction of emotional distress, and for defamation.

JURISDICTION

1. This Court has subject matter jurisdiction pursuant to (a) 28 U.S.C. §1331, because the case arises under the Constitution and laws of the United States; (b) 28 U.S.C. §1343, because this action seeks redress and damages for violation of 42 U.S.C. §§1983 and 1985 and, in particular, the due process and equal protection provisions of the United States Constitution, including the rights protected in the Fifth and Fourteenth Amendments thereof; and (c) 28 U.S.C. §1232, since there is diversity of citizenship and this is a civil action involving, exclusive of interest and costs, a sum in excess of $50,000.00. This Court also has jurisdiction over the causes of action alleged in Counts III and IV pursuant to federal pendant jurisdiction.

VENUE

2. Venue is appropriate in this judicial district under 28 U.S.C. §1391(b), because Defendants William Jefferson Clinton and Danny Ferguson reside here, and a substantial part of the events giving rise to this Complaint occurred here.

THE PARTIES

3. Plaintiff Paula Corbin Jones (hereafter "Jones") is a citizen of the State of California. Prior to her marriage on December 28, 1991, Plaintiff was known as Paula Rosalee Corbin.

4. Defendant William Jefferson Clinton (hereafter "Clinton") is a citizen of the State of Arkansas or alternatively of the District of Columbia.

5. Defendant Danny Ferguson (hereafter "Ferguson") is a citizen of the State of Arkansas.

FACTS

6. On or about March 11, 1991, Jones began work as an Arkansas State employee for the Arkansas Industrial Development Commission (hereafter "AIDC"), an agency within the executive branch of the State of Arkansas. The Governor of Arkansas is the chief executive officer of the executive branch of the State of Arkansas.

7. On May 8, 1991, the AIDC sponsored the Third Annual Governor's Quality Management Conference (hereafter "Conference"), which was held at the Excelsior Hotel in Little Rock, Arkansas. Clinton, then Governor of Arkansas, delivered a speech at the Conference on that day.

8. Also on that day, Jones worked at the registration desk at the Conference along with Pamela Blackard (hereafter "Blackard") another AIDC employee.

9. A man approached the registration desk and informed Jones and Blackard that he was Trooper Danny Ferguson, Bill Clinton's bodyguard. Defendant Ferguson was at that time a law enforcement officer within the ranks of the Arkansas State Police and assigned to the Governor's Security Detail. He was in street clothes and displayed a firearm on his person. He made small talk with Jones and Blackard and then left.

10. At approximately 2:30 p.m. on that day, Ferguson reappeared at the registration desk, delivered a piece of paper to Jones with a four digit number written on it and said: "The Governor would like to meet with you" in this suite number. Plaintiff had never met Defendant Clinton and saw him in person for the first time at the Conference.

11. A three-way conversation followed between Ferguson, Blackard and Jones about what the Governor could want. Jones, who was then a rank-and-file Arkansas state employee being paid approximately $6.35 an hour, thought it was an honor to be asked to meet the Governor. Ferguson stated during the conversation: "It's okay, we do this all the time for the Governor."

12. Jones agreed to meet with the Governor because she thought it might lead to an enhanced employment opportunity with the State. Blackard told Jones that she would assume Plaintiff's duties at the registration desk.

13. Trooper Ferguson then escorted Jones to the floor of the hotel suite whose number had been written on the slip of paper Trooper Ferguson had given to Jones. The door was slightly ajar when she arrived at the suite.

14. Jones knocked on the door frame and Clinton answered. Plaintiff entered. Ferguson remained outside.

15. The room was furnished as a business suite, not for an overnight hotel guest. It contained a couch and chairs, but no bed.

16. Clinton shook Jones' hand, invited her in, and closed the door.

17. A few minutes of small talk ensued, which included asking Jones about her job. Clinton told Jones that Dave Harrington is "my good friend." On May 8, 1991, David Harrington was Director of the AIDC, having been appointed to that post by Governor Clinton. Harrington was Jones' ultimate superior within the AIDC.

18. Clinton then took Jones' hand and pulled her toward him, so that their bodies were in close proximity.

19. Jones removed her hand from his and retreated several feet.

20. However, Clinton approached Jones again. He said: "I love the way your hair flows down your back" and "I love your curves." While saying these things, Clinton put his hand on Plaintiff's leg and started sliding it toward the hem of Plaintiff's culottes. Clinton also bent down to attempt to kiss Jones on the neck.

21. Jones exclaimed, "What are you doing?" and escaped from Clinton's physical proximity by walking away from him. Jones tried to distract Clinton by chatting with him about his wife. Jones later took a seat at the end of the sofa nearest the door. Clinton asked Jones: "Are you married?" She responded that she had a regular boyfriend. Clinton then approached the sofa and as he sat down he lowered his trousers and underwear exposing his erect penis and asked Jones to "kiss it."

22. There were distinguishing characteristics in Clinton's genital area that were obvious to Jones.

23. Jones became horrified, jumped up from the couch, stated that she was "not that kind of girl" and said: "Look, I've got to go." She attempted to explain that she would get in trouble for being away from the registration desk.

24. Clinton, while fondling his penis said: "Well, I don't want to make you do anything you don't want to do." Clinton then stood up and pulled up his pants and said: "If you get in trouble for leaving work, have Dave call me immediately and I'll take care of it." As Jones left the room Clinton looked sternly at Jones and said: "You are smart. Let's keep this between ourselves."

25. Jones believed "Dave" to be the same David Harrington, of whom Clinton previously referred. Clinton, by his comments about Harrington to Jones, affirmed that he had control over Jones' employment, and that he was willing to use that power. Jones became fearful that her refusal to succumb to Clinton's advances could damage her in her job and even jeopardize her employment.

26. At no time, nor in any manner, did Jones encourage Clinton to turn the meeting toward a sexual liaison. To the contrary, the unwanted sexual advances made by Clinton were repugnant and abhorrent to Jones who took all reasonable steps she could think to do to terminate Clinton's perverse attention and actions toward her.

27. Jones left the hotel suite and came into the presence of Trooper Ferguson in the hallway. Ferguson did not escort Plaintiff back to the registration desk. Jones said nothing to Ferguson and he said nothing to her during her departure from the suite.

28. Jones was visibly shaken and upset when she returned to the registration desk. Pamela Blackard immediately asked her what was wrong. After a moment, during which Jones attempted to collect herself, she told Blackard much of what had happened. Blackard attempted to comfort Plaintiff.

29. Jones thereafter left the Conference and went to the work place of her friend, Debra Ballentine.

30. When Ballentine met Plaintiff at the reception area, she immediately asked Jones what was wrong because Jones was visibly upset and nervous. Plaintiff wanted to talk about something that just happened and wanted to discuss it someplace privately. Ballentine and Jones went to a private area in the office, and later outside. Jones then told Ballentine what had happened with Clinton in the hotel suite. According to Ballentine, Jones told her that Clinton said as she left the room, "I know you're a smart girl and I'm sure you'll keep this to yourself."

31. Ballentine urged Jones to report the incident. Plaintiff refused, fearing that, if she did so, no one would believe her account, that she would lose her job, and that the incident would endanger her relationship with her then-fiance (now husband), Stephen Jones.

32. Later, on the same day, Plaintiff also described the substance of her encounter with Clinton to her sister, Charlotte Corbin Brown.

33. Within two days of May 8, 1991, Plaintiff also informed her sister, Lydia Corbin Cathey, and her mother, Delmar Lee Corbin, the substance of her encounter with Clinton.

34. Plaintiff also told her fiance, Stephen Jones, that "Bill Clinton made a pass at me but I said 'no'." She, however, did not at that time tell him the lurid details of her horrific encounter with Clinton in the hotel suite, which she feared, if disclosed, might ruin her relationship with Mr. Jones.

35. Plaintiff continued to work at AIDC. One of her duties was to deliver documents to and from the Office of the Governor, as well as other offices within the Arkansas State Capitol complex. In or about June, 1991, while Jones was performing this duty, Ferguson saw her at the Governor's office and said: "Bill wants your phone number. Hillary's out of town often and Bill would like to see you." Plaintiff refused to provide her telephone number.

36. On another occasion, Ferguson approached Jones and asked: "How's Steve?" This frightened Plaintiff and made her feel as if she was being watched and was not safe. She had never told Ferguson or Clinton the name of her fiance.

37. Plaintiff and Stephen Jones later married. She gave birth to her child and returned to work, after which she encountered Ferguson at Governor Clinton's office. Ferguson told her: "I've told Bill how good looking you are since you've had the baby." This, too, frightened Plaintiff and made her feel that her activities were being monitored.

38. On one occasion, Plaintiff was accosted by Clinton in the Rotunda of the Arkansas State Capitol. Clinton draped his arm over Plaintiff, pulled her close and tightly to his body and said: "Don't we make a beautiful couple -- beauty and the beast?" Clinton directed this remark to his bodyguard, Trooper Larry Patterson, an officer of the Arkansas State Police and also a member of the Governor's Security Detail.

39. Jones continued to work at AIDC even though she was in constant fear that Governor Clinton might take retaliatory action against her because of her rejection of his abhorrent sexual advances. Her enjoyment of her work was severely diminished. In fact, she was treated in a hostile and rude manner by certain superiors in AIDC. This rude conduct had not happened prior to her encounter with Clinton. Further, after her maternity leave she was transferred to a position which had no responsible duties for which she could be adequately evaluated to earn advancement. The reason

given to her by her superiors for the transfer was that her previous position had been eliminated. This reason was untrue since her former position was not abolished. It was a pretext for the real reason which was that she was being punished for her rejection of the various advances made by Clinton described above. In addition, the job in which she was placed called for a higher grade and pay, yet she was not paid more money than she received in her previous position. Although other employees received merit increases, Jones never received a raise beyond a cost of living increase.

40. Jones terminated her employment and separated from AIDC service on February 20, 1993. On May 4, 1993, Plaintiff, her husband and child moved to California.

41. In January, 1994, Plaintiff visited her family and friends in Arkansas. While Jones was in Arkansas, Ms. Ballentine telephoned Jones to arrange a meeting for lunch. During the telephone conversation, Ballentine read to Plaintiff a paragraph from an article published in the January, 1994 issue of _The American Spectator_ magazine regarding Plaintiff's hotel suite encounter with Clinton. Attached hereto, and incorporated herein, as Exhibit "A" is a copy of _The American Spectator_ article.

42. _The American Spectator_ account asserts that a woman by the name of "Paula" told an unnamed trooper (obviously Defendant Ferguson), who had escorted "Paula" to Clinton's hotel room, that "she was available to be Clinton's regular girlfriend if he so desired," thus implying a consummated and satisfying sexual

encounter with Clinton, as well as a willingness to continue a sexual relationship with him. These assertions are untrue. The article, using information apparently derived from Ferguson, also incorrectly asserts that the encounter took place in the evening.

43. The American Spectator account also asserted that the troopers' "'official' duties included facilitating Clinton's cheating on his wife. This meant that, on the State payroll, and using State time, vehicles and resources, they were instructed by Clinton on a regular basis to approach women and to solicit their telephone numbers for the Governor, to drive him in State vehicles to rendezvous points and guard him during sexual encounters; to secure hotel rooms and other meeting places for sex; ..." and various other things to facilitate Clinton's sex life including "to help Clinton cover-up his activities by keeping tabs on Hillary's whereabouts and lying to Hillary about her husband's whereabouts." Although this pattern of conduct by Clinton may be true, the magazine article concluded, evidently from interviews with troopers from Clinton's Security Detail, including Ferguson, that "all of the women appear to have been willing participants in the affairs and liaisons [emphasis added]."

44. Since Jones ("Paula") was one of the women preyed upon by Clinton and his troopers, including by Defendant Ferguson, in the manner described above, those who read this magazine account could conclude falsely that Jones ("Paula") had a sexual relationship and affair with Clinton. Jones' reputation within her community was thus seriously damaged.

45. Jones realized that those persons who already knew about the hotel room encounter could identify her as the "Paula" mentioned in The American Spectator article. She became extremely upset because, *inter alia*, she feared that the statements in the magazine would damage her relationship with her husband, her family, and her friends and acquaintances, some of whom might have believed that she had agreed to be Clinton's "girlfriend" at a time when she was engaged to Mr. Jones.

46. On January 8, 1994, at approximately 12:00 noon, Jones and Ballentine were dining at the Golden Corral Steakhouse in North Little Rock, Arkansas. Trooper Ferguson, who happened to be dining with his wife at this restaurant, came over to their table to talk to Jones. Since Jones believed that the ultimate source of the report in The American Spectator of the hotel suite encounter was Trooper Ferguson, she confronted him on this matter. Trooper Ferguson stated that he was sorry that Jones' first name had appeared in the magazine article but that he had purposely concealed her last name and place of employment from those to whom he recounted the incident. Trooper Ferguson also said that he knew Jones had rebuffed Mr. Clinton's sexual advances because, "Clinton told me you wouldn't do anything anyway, Paula."

47. Because the false statements appearing in The American Spectator article that Jones was willing to have sex with Clinton (and the innuendo that she had already done so when she left the hotel suite) threatened her marriage, her friendships, and her family relationships, Plaintiff spoke publicly on February 11,

1994, that she was the "Paula" mentioned in The American Spectator article, that she had rebuffed Clinton's sexual advances, and that she had not expressed a willingness to be his girlfriend. Jones and her lawyer asked that Clinton acknowledge the incident, state that Jones had rejected Clinton's advances, and apologize to Jones.

48. Clinton, who is now President of the United States of America responded to Jones' request for an apology by having his press spokespersons deliver a statement on his behalf that the incident never happened, and that he never met Plaintiff. Thus, by innuendo and effect, Clinton publicly branded Plaintiff a liar. Moreover, as recently as the week this Complaint was filed, Clinton, through his White House aides, stated that Plaintiff's account of the hotel room incident was untrue and a "cheap political trick."

49. Clinton hired an attorney, who, as Clinton's agent, said that Jones' account "is really just another effort to rewrite the results of the election [i.e. for President of the United States] and ... distract the President from his agenda." The attorney further asked the question: "Why are these claims being brought now, three years after the fact?" The attorney also asked how Jones' allegations could be taken "seriously." These comments by Clinton's counsel, on behalf of Clinton, imply that Jones is a liar.

50. Dee Dee Meyers, White House Spokeswoman, said of Jones' allegations: "It's just not true." Thus, the pattern of defaming Jones continues to this date.

51. Clinton knows that Jones' allegations are true and that his, and his attorney's, spokespersons', and agents' denials are false.

52. The outrageous nature of Clinton's branding of Jones as a liar is aggravated in that a greater stigma and reputation loss is suffered by Jones by the statements of the President of the United States in whom the general public reposes trust and confidence in the integrity of the holder of that office.

53. Clinton, a member of the Arkansas State Bar, knew or should have known on May 8, 1991, and thereafter, that Arkansas law provides that harassment, including the touching or attempt or threat to do so which subjects the victim to offensive or potentially offensive physical contact, is a criminal violation of Arkansas Code Annotated 5-71-208.

54. While Jones was in Clinton's hotel suite, Jones was falsely imprisoned by Clinton's intentional restriction of her personal freedom of movement without legal right. Clinton's use of force in pulling Jones toward him, his words and acts, and the armed police guard outside the door, in conjunction with the impressive atmosphere of her being alone with the Governor of the State who was also her superior's boss, caused her to be initially and temporarily afraid to terminate the meeting.

55. The statements, acts, and omissions of Clinton's agents, servants, and employees who acted under his explicit and implicit instructions and supervision, during the pertinent periods herein when he was Governor of Arkansas, and after he became President,

bind Clinton under the doctrines of agency, joint conduct, master-servant, respondeat superior, and conspiracy.

56. The actions of the Arkansas state employees, including Defendant Ferguson and other agents of Clinton were taken under color of state law.

57. Clinton's actions and omissions above stated caused Jones embarrassment, humiliation, fear, emotional distress, horror, grief, shame, marital discord and loss of reputation.

COUNT I

DEPRIVATION OF CONSTITUTIONAL RIGHTS AND PRIVILEGES (42 U.S.C. §1983)

58. Plaintiff incorporates by reference paragraphs 1 through 57.

59. Plaintiff is entitled to the equal protection of the laws under the Fourteenth Amendment of the United States Constitution, and due process of law under the Fifth and Fourteenth Amendments of the United States Constitution.

60. Defendant Clinton, as Governor of Arkansas, acting under color of state law, discriminated against Plaintiff because of her gender by sexually harassing and assaulting her on May 8, 1991, and thereafter, and this deprived Jones of her right to equal protection of the law.

61. Further, he continued personally, and through agents, to impose a hostile work environment on Plaintiff in which she feared the loss of her employment and the possible adverse employment

actions against her, including job discrimination and monitoring of her personal life. As described above she was placed in a category separate from other public employees in that she was actually subjected to hostility by her superiors, which deprived her of an opportunity for advancement and she suffered an economic depravation.

62. Plaintiff, as a citizen and Arkansas state employee, was entitled to due process protection of freedom from arbitrary action which jeopardized her property interest in her public employee job in that she should not have been subjected arbitrarily to the fear of losing that job or of having to provide sex to the Governor as a quid pro quo for keeping the job. Further, she should not have been subjected arbitrarily to the fear of losing the enjoyment of a proper and pleasant work environment, or to other adverse actions which she feared and which deprived her of the proper enjoyment and efficiency of her work. Clinton's actions deprived Jones of her due process liberty and property interests guaranteed to her by the Constitution of the United States.

63. Plaintiff also was entitled to a due process liberty interest in her reputation as an honest public employee. Clinton's actions and statements deprived Jones of these rights.

64. Plaintiff, for a brief period of time, was held against her will by the oppressive atmosphere of intimidation caused by the presence of the highest official of the State of Arkansas and an armed guard at the door. Not only was she subjected to unwelcome sexual advances, but also was personally restrained and imprisoned

by the seizing of her person, against her will, by Clinton and his agent.

65. The above-described actions of Clinton were undertaken when he was acting under the color of state law, as Governor of Arkansas, and said actions deprived Jones of federal equal protection and due process rights guaranteed by the Fifth and Fourteenth Amendments of the United States Constitution, and made actionable by 42 U.S.C. § 1983 (The Civil Rights Act).

COUNT II

CONSPIRACY TO DEPRIVING PERSONS OF EQUAL PROTECTION OF THE LAWS (42 U.S.C. § 1985)

66. Plaintiff incorporates by reference paragraphs 1 through 65.

67. Clinton conspired with his Security Detail, including with Defendant Ferguson, and perhaps with others currently unknown to this Plaintiff, to deprive Jones of equal protection of the laws and of equal privileges and immunities under the laws, as further set forth in Count I above.

68. The conspirators committed some acts in furtherance of the conspiracy which included contacting Jones and bringing her to Clinton on May 8, 1991 to permit him to attempt to entice her on to have a sexual liaison with him.

69. As a result of the conspiracy, Jones was injured by Defendants in her person and property and deprived of having and exercising her rights and privileges as a citizen of the United States, as is more fully set forth in Count I.

COUNT III
INTENTIONAL INFLICTION OF EMOTIONAL DISTRESS

70. Plaintiff incorporates by reference paragraphs 1 through 69.

71. The conduct of Clinton herein set forth was odious, perverse and outrageous. Not only were the acts of sexual perversity unwelcome by Jones, but they were wilful, wanton, reckless, intentional, persistent and continuous in the hotel room.

72. Clinton's sexual advances, assaults upon and imprisonment of Jones' person, and his exposure of his erect penis and his requests of acts to be performed thereupon were extreme, intentional, and caused Jones severe emotional distress.

73. Not content with the events in the hotel on May 8, 1991, Clinton on subsequent occasions, acting himself and through his agents, as specified above, aggravated further the initial severe emotional damage to Jones.

74. These actions were so outrageous in character, and extreme in degree, as to go beyond all possible bounds of decency, and to be regarded as atrocious and utterly intolerable in a civilized society.

COUNT IV
DEFAMATION

75. Plaintiff incorporates by reference paragraphs 1 through 74.

76. On several occasions on and after February 11, 1994, Clinton, and his agents and employees acting pursuant to his direction, maliciously and wilfully, defamed Jones by making statements which Clinton knew to be false. These statements were made with the intent and certain knowledge that they would be reprinted in the print and other media.

77. Such statements by Clinton, his agents and employees, characterized Jones as a liar and as being "pathetic," and damaged her good name, character, and reputation.

78. Defendant Ferguson's statements likewise maliciously and willfully defamed plaintiff and damaged her good name, character and reputation. Ferguson's statement that Jones had agreed to be Clinton's girlfriend, and his innuendo that she had willingly participated in a sexual encounter, were knowingly false.

79. That Ferguson knew these statements were false is confirmed by Clinton's denial to Ferguson that anything happened of a sexual nature between Clinton and Jones.

RELIEF REQUESTED

WHEREFORE, Plaintiff requests the following relief:

a. Count I, judgment against Defendant Clinton for compensatory damages of $ 75,000.00; punitive damages for Defendant's wilful, outrageous and malicious conduct, of $100,000.00; the costs of her suit and attorneys' fees; nominal damages, and such other and further relief as the Court may deem proper.

b. Count II, judgment against Defendant Clinton and

Defendant Ferguson, jointly and severally for compensatory damages of $ 75,000.00; punitive damages for Defendant's wilful, outrageous and malicious conduct, of $ 100,000.00; the costs of her suit and attorney's fees; nominal damages, and such other and further relief as the Court may deem proper.

c. Count III, judgment against Defendant Clinton for compensatory damages of $ 75,000.00; punitive damages for Defendant's wilful, outrageous and malicious statements and conduct, of $ 100,000.00; the costs of her suit and attorneys' fees; nominal damages, and such other and further relief as the Court may deem proper.

d. Count IV, judgment against Defendant Clinton and Defendant Ferguson, jointly and severally for compensatory damages of $ 75,000.00; punitive damages for Defendant's wilful, outrageous and malicious statements and conduct, of $ 100,000.00; the costs of her suit and attorneys' fees; nominal damages, and such other and further relief as the Court may deem proper.

JURY TRIAL DEMANDED

Plaintiff demands a trial by jury on each of the counts.

Respectfully Submitted,

PAULA CORBIN JONES
By Her Counsel

Gilbert K. Davis, VA Bar No. 4683
Attorney for Plantiff
9516-C Lee Highway
Fairfax, Virginia 22031
(703) 352-3850

and

Joseph Cammarata, VA Bar No. 35118
Attorney for Plaintiff
9516-C Lee Highway
Fairfax, Virginia 22031
(703) 352-3850

VERIFICATION

I hereby certify under penalty of perjury that I am the Plaintiff in the above-captioned case; that I have read the foregoing Complaint; and, that the facts related therein are true and correct to the best of my knowledge, information, and belief.

Paula Corbin Jones

Appendix B **Civil Rights Complaint** - Webster Bivens v. Six Unknown Named Agents of the Federal Narcotic Bureau

In The United States District Court
For the Eastern District of New York

Webster Bivens,
Plaintiff

vs. Civil No. 67G 655

Six Unknown Named
Agents of the Federal
Narcotics Bureau,
Defendants

Complaint

COMES NOW, Webster Bivens, Plaintiff in the above-entitled cause, depose and says:

1. This Court has jurisdiction to entertain this complaint under the Civil Rights Act of 1871, Title 42 U.S.C., Section 1983, and Title 28 U.S.C., Sections 1331(a) and 1343(3) and (4).

2. While acting under the colors and authority of the United States of America, six (6) agents of the U.S. Narcotic Bureau, did violate Plaintiff's constitutional rights, the facts are as follows:

Facts

1. Plaintiff is, and at all times pertinent to this action, has been a citizen of the United States.

2. Each of the Defendants is, and at all time pertinent to this action has been an agent of the Federal Narcotic Bureau, of the United States and was acting under color of authority of the laws of the United States.

3. On November 26, 1965, Plaintiff was in his apartment at 574 Taylor Avenue, Bronx, New York City, when Defendants entered said apartment, searched it and placed Plaintiff under arrest for violation of narcotics laws.

4. Neither of the Defendants ever had any warrants to enter Plaintiff's apartment or search the same, nor did either of them have any warrant to arrest Plaintiff.

5. Defendants used unreasonable force in effecting the arrest and restraint of Plaintiff at his apartment and the search of Plaintiff's apartment and his arrest were conducted in an unreasonable manner.

6. In the course of the arrest and restraint of Plaintiff, he was manacled in the presence of his children and wife, and threatened with arrest of his entire family.

7. After being arrested by the Defendants, Plaintiff was taken to the Federal Narcotic Bureau, then to the Federal Court Building, Eastern District, Brooklyn, New York. At the Federal Narcotic Bureau, 90 Church Street, New York City, Plaintiff was interrogated and fingerprinted, photographed and subsequently booked. He was also subjected to a search of his person and visual search of his private parts.

8. The events above described caused Plaintiff great humiliation, embarrassment and mental suffering; and will, in the future, continue to cause him such humiliation, embarrassment and mental suffering.

9. All of the events which followed Plaintiff's arrest at his apartment were proximately caused by the acts of the Defendants in unlawfully searching Plaintiff's apartment, and in unlawfully placing him under arrest.

10. That the acts were done unlawfully, unreasonably and contrary to law and caused Plaintiff humiliation, embarrassment and mental anguish and will in the future continue to do so as a consequence of the unlawful search and arrest by the Defendants, makes the Plaintiff entitled to the just compensation of $150,000 dollars from each of the Defendants and any and all other such other relief as this Court deems just and proper.

Respectfully submitted,

/s/ ____________________

Webster Bivens, Pro-Se

Appendix C **Civil Rights Complaint (Title 42 U.S. Code Section 1983)** - Haupt v. Dillard

[C]

William F. Gary
Glenn Klein
HARRANG, LONG, WATKINSON,
ARNOLD & LAIRD, P.C.
101 E. Broadway, Suite 400
Eugene, Oregon 97401
(503)485-0220

J. Pat Horton
HORTON & KOENIG
96 E. Broadway, Suite 5
Eugene, Oregon 97401
(503)344-2791

Of Attorneys for Plaintiff

IN THE UNITED STATES DISTRICT COURT

FOR THE DISTRICT OF NEVADA

HOWARD L. HAUPT, Plaintiff, v. T.D. DILLARD; ROBERT LEONARD; LAS VEGAS METROPOLITAN POLICE DEPARTMENT; CITY OF LAS VEGAS, NEVADA; CLARK COUNTY, NEVADA, Defendants.	CV-S-90-121-PMP-RJJ Civil Case No. COMPLAINT (Civil Rights Violations and Related State Law Claims) JURY DEMAND

NATURE OF THE CASE

This is an action for money damages against the Las Vegas Metropolitan Police Department, (Metro), Metro Officers T.D. Dillard and Robert Leonard, the City of Las Vegas, Nevada, and Clark County, Nevada, for violations of the Plaintiff's civil rights.

On February 19, 1988 Plaintiff was charged by the Defendants with the kidnapping and the capital murder of

HORTON & KOENIG
ATTORNEYS AT LAW
96 E. BROADWAY — SUITE 5
EUGENE, OREGON 97401
(503) 344-2791

Alexander Harris, a seven year old child. Defendants caused Plaintiff to remain incarcerated for a period of approximately 13 days, publicly accusing Plaintiff of the crimes for which he was charged above. Plaintiff was tried and acquitted of all charges. During the investigation and prosecution of Plaintiff, Defendants fabricated evidence against Plaintiff by pressuring witnesses to identify Plaintiff as the kidnapper and killer of Alexander Harris; falsified search and arrest warrants; withheld exculpatory information to issuing magistrates which showed the innocence of the Plaintiff; and denied Plaintiff counsel during an interrogation incident to his unlawful arrest. During the trial, the Defendants, including Metro, threatened and intimidated the trial court judge into not giving advisory jury instructions of acquittal.

The Defendants conspired among themselves and with others throughout the course of the investigation and trial to deprive the Plaintiff of his constitutional rights.

Metro, the City, and County, were well aware of Dillard and Leonard's previous conduct in other similar type cases which resulted in deprivation of constitutional rights to other individuals.

The Defendants' conduct was intentional and malicious; caused Plaintiff to suffer loss of employment, lost wages, and extreme emotional distress; subjected the Plaintiff to humiliation and public embarrassment; and deprived Plaintiff of his constitutional rights.

HORTON & KOENIG
ATTORNEYS AT LAW
96 E. BROADWAY — SUITE 5
EUGENE, OREGON 97401
(503) 344-2791

PLAINTIFF ALLEGES:

JURISDICTION AND VENUE

(1) This action is brought pursuant to 42 U.S.C. §§ 1983 and 1988, and the Fourteenth Amendment to the United States Constitution. Jurisdiction is founded upon 28 U.S.C. §§ 1331, 1332 and 1343. Plaintiff further invokes the Court's pendent jurisdiction to hear claims arising under state law. The amount in controversy exceeds $10,000.

(2) The material actions occurred in Clark County, Nevada, or Southern California. Therefore, venue is proper in the Southern Division of Nevada District.

PARTIES

(3) Plaintiff Howard L. Haupt is, and at all material times was, a citizen of the United States and a resident of San Diego, California.

(4) Defendants Dillard and Leonard are, and at all material times were, duly appointed police officers of Defendant Las Vegas Metropolitan Police Department and citizens of Nevada for purposes of diversity jurisdiction. Defendants Las Vegas Metropolitan Police Department, City of Las Vegas, and Clark County, were and are political subdivisions of the State of Nevada and citizens thereof for the purposes of diversity jurisdiction. At all material times, all Defendants were acting under color of state law.

///

///

HORTON & KOENIG
ATTORNEYS AT LAW
96 E. BROADWAY — SUITE 5
EUGENE, OREGON 97401
(503) 344-2791

GENERAL ALLEGATIONS

(5) On November 27, 1987, Alexander Harris, a seven year old child, was reported missing from the arcade at Whiskey Pete's Hotel and Casino in Stateline, Nevada. On December 30, 1987, the child was found dead beneath the hotel manager's trailer at Whiskey Pete's Hotel and Casino.

(6) A replay of the videotape of the arcade from the day Alexander Harris was reported missing showed that a child similar in appearance to Alexander Harris was present. Also present in the arcade were three male adults. Defendants obtained photographs of males who were guests at Whiskey Pete's the day Alexander was reported missing. Those photographs were shown to four witnesses who recalled seeing a little boy in the company of a man the day that Alexander Harris was reported missing.

(8) None of the witnesses selected Plaintiff's picture. One witness stated that Plaintiff definitely was not the man she saw. Two other witnesses both identified the same individual -- someone other than Plaintiff -- as the person they saw with the boy. Another witness described an individual -- whose description did not match Plaintiffs -- with the boy. Despite these reactions and descriptions, Defendants conspired to arrest and prosecute Plaintiff for the kidnapping and murder of Alexander Harris.

(9) After repeatedly showing Plaintiff's picture to the witnesses, Defendants transported the witnesses to Plaintiff's

HORTON & KOENIG
ATTORNEYS AT LAW
96 E. BROADWAY — SUITE 5
EUGENE, OREGON 97401
(503) 344-2791

place of work in San Diego. Defendants asked the witnesses to point out any person who looked familiar. The witnesses identified Plaintiff as a person who looked familiar.

(10) After Defendants had the witnesses view Plaintiff in person, Defendants again asked the witnesses to look at photographs of men as described above. The witnesses then selected Plaintiff's photograph as the assailant.

(11) The Defendants created a suggestive environment calculated to induce witnesses to identify Plaintiff, even though Defendants knew or had reason to know that Plaintiff was not responsible for the crime.

(12) Defendants sought and obtained between February 16 and 19, 1988, both search and arrest warrants. In doing so, Defendants intentionally and in bad faith filed false and misleading affidavits in support of the warrants. Defendants intentionally and in bad faith failed to inform the magistrate of exculpatory information showing the innocence of the Plaintiff.

(13) On February 19, 1988, Defendants arrested Plaintiff as he was leaving his place of employment. Defendants continued interrogating Plaintiff after Plaintiff had invoked his Fifth and Sixth Amendment rights to remain silent and to have the assistance of counsel. Notwithstanding Defendants' attempts to coerce Plaintiff to confess to crimes of kidnapping and murder, Plaintiff steadfastly maintained his innocence. Additionally, Defendants made no effort to corroborate the

HORTON & KOENIG
ATTORNEYS AT LAW
96 E. BROADWAY – SUITE 5
EUGENE, OREGON 97401
(503) 344-2791

alibi witnesses Plaintiff offered who could substantiate Plaintiff's claim that he was not at Whiskey Pete's at the time the child was kidnapped or reported missing.

(14) Plaintiff was confined in jail until March 4, 1988, when he was freed on bail. During this time, Defendants published or caused to be published false and defamatory statements of the Plaintiff's guilt and bad character. Defendants made the statements knowing they were false, or alternatively, with reckless disregard of their truth or falsity.

(15) On January 9, 1989, Plaintiff's trial commenced. After approximately five weeks of testimony, the Court and counsel discussed possible jury instructions. The Court indicated that it was inclined to give an advisory instruction of acquittal.

(16) The District Attorney responded by personally attacking the judge in a verbally abusive manner.

(17) The District Attorney then informed Defendant Dillard that the Court intended to give the advisory instruction of innocence. Thereafter, Defendant Dillard personally telephoned the judge to intimidate and implicitly to threaten the judge into not giving the jury instruction.

(18) Defendant Leonard was present in court immediately after Defendant Dillard telephoned the judge, in order further to intimidate the Court into not giving the advisory jury instruction of acquittal.

HORTON & KOENIG
ATTORNEYS AT LAW
96 E. BROADWAY — SUITE 5
EUGENE, OREGON 97401
(503) 344-2791

(19) Metro has engaged in a pattern of attempting to influence the neutrality of the Las Vegas Courts in the past and in this case unlawfully conspired to influence the Court into denying Plaintiff's right to receive a fair and impartial trial.

(20) Based on the intentional and unlawful conduct of Defendants, the Court did not give the instruction of acquittal. On February 15, 1989, the jury returned a verdict of not guilty.

(21) The prosecution of Plaintiff was procured by false and misleading information that suggested that probable cause existed to prosecute, when in fact it did not.

(22) The actions of Defendants Dillard and Leonard, as alleged herein, were intentional, and Defendant Dillard's and Leonard's actions were consistent with a pattern of unlawful and unconstitutional actions undertaken by them in previous cases. Other suits had been filed against Defendants Dillard, Leonard, Metro, City and County because of Defendant Dillard's and Leonard's unconstitutional conduct. Metro, the City and the County, knew, or should have known, of Defendants Dillard's and Leonard's unconstitutional conduct, and failed to prevent Defendant Dillard and Leonard from taking similar action against Plaintiff.

(23) Metro had a policy of intimidating State Court Judges to deprive Defendants in criminal cases of the right to a fair trial.

HORTON & KOENIG
ATTORNEYS AT LAW
96 E. BROADWAY — SUITE 5
EUGENE, OREGON 97401
(503) 344-2791

(24) As a direct and proximate result of Defendants' actions, Plaintiff was deprived of his liberty, was forced to incur legal fees and expenses in defense of the prosecution in excess of $300,000.00, lost income in excess of $5,000.00, suffered great mental anguish and extreme emotional distress, and was greatly humiliated.

FIRST CLAIM FOR RELIEF

(Deprivation of Civil Rights)

(25) Plaintiff realleges paragraphs 1 through 24 above.

(26) The actions alleged above deprived Plaintiff of the following rights under the United States Constitution:

a. Freedom from capricious and malicious prosecution;

b. Freedom from unduly suggestive photo identifications;

c. Freedom from unreasonable searches and seizures;

d. Right to have an attorney present during an interrogation; and

e. Right to a fair and impartial trial.

(27) Pursuant to 42 U.S.C. §§ 1988, Plaintiff is entitled to reasonable attorney fees.

SECOND CLAIM FOR RELIEF

(Conspiracy to Deprive Civil Rights)

(28) Plaintiff realleges paragraphs 1 through 24 above.

(29) Defendant police officers conspired with the

HORTON & KOENIG
ATTORNEYS AT LAW
96 E. BROADWAY — SUITE 5
EUGENE, OREGON 97401
(503) 344-2791

District Attorney and others to deprive Plaintiff of his right to a fair and impartial trial.

(30) Defendant police officers further conspired among themselves and with others to deprive Plaintiff of the following rights under the United States Constitution:

a. Freedom from capricious and malicious prosecution;

b. Freedom from unduly suggestive photo identifications;

c. Freedom from unreasonable searches and seizures; and

d. Right to have an attorney present during police interrogation.

(31) Pursuant to 42 U.S.C. § 1988, Plaintiff is entitled to attorney fees.

THIRD CLAIM FOR RELIEF

(False Imprisonment)

(32) Plaintiff realleges paragraphs 1 through 24 above.

(33) As summarized above, Defendants unlawfully detained or caused the detention of Plaintiff.

FOURTH CLAIM FOR RELIEF

(Intentional Infliction of Emotional Distress)

(34) Plaintiff realleges paragraphs 1 through 24 above.

(35) At all times material herein, the acts and omissions of Defendants were undertaken with deliberate intention to cause Plaintiff to suffer extreme emotional distress.

HORTON & KOENIG
ATTORNEYS AT LAW
96 E. BROADWAY — SUITE 5
EUGENE, OREGON 97401
(503) 344-2791

(36) As a result of Defendants' acts and omissions as summarized above, Plaintiff did suffer extreme emotional distress.

FIFTH CLAIM FOR RELIEF

(Defamation)

(37) Plaintiff realleges paragraphs 1 through 24 above.

(38) Between February 1988 and February 1989, Defendants made or caused to be made to third parties, including news media, false statements of material fact concerning Plaintiff, to the effect Plaintiff was a child murderer even though no legal adjudication had been made to that effect. Their statements were designed to deny the Plaintiff a fair and impartial trial.

(39) Defendants made or caused to be made the above-referenced false statements intentionally, knowingly or with reckless disregard for the truth or falsity of such statements.

(40) The above-referenced statements made by Defendants concerning the Plaintiff were false and defamatory in nature, and intended to hold and did hold Plaintiff up to public contempt, ridicule, hatred and harassment, all to Plaintiff's damage.

WHEREFORE, Plaintiff prays for judgment as follows:

a. Compensatory and consequential damages against each and every Defendant in the amount of $3,000,000.00;

b. Punitive damages against each Defendant police officer in the amount of $1,000,000.00;

HORTON & KOENIG
ATTORNEYS AT LAW
96 E. BROADWAY — SUITE 5
EUGENE, OREGON 97401
(503) 344-2791

c. Attorney fees incurred herein against each and every Defendant; and

d. Such other additional relief as the Court may deem just and equitable.

DATED this 31 day of January, 1990.

Respectfully submitted,

HARRANG, LONG, WATKINSON, ARNOLD, LAIRD, P.C.

By: [signature]
William F. Gary, OSB #77032
Glenn Klein, OSB #83110

HORTON & KOENIG

By: [signature]
J. Pat Horton, OSB #67052

HORTON & KOENIG
ATTORNEYS AT LAW
96 E. BROADWAY — SUITE 5
EUGENE, OREGON 97401
(503) 344-2791

Appendix D **Application for a Writ of Mandamus** - Laroy D. Cox v. O'Malley, et. al.

[D]

UNITED STATES COURT OF APPEALS FOR THE
FIRST CIRCUIT

NO.

UNITED STATES DISTRICT COURT
FOR THE DISTRICT OF MASSACHUSETTS

	C.A. NO. 93-10632H
LAROY D. COX Plaintiff v. PETER J. O'MALLEY, MILLER THOMAS, JR TRENT W. HOLLAND, WILLIAM DUNN, FRANCIS M. ROACHE, individually and in their official capacities, CITY OF BOSTON, AND OTHER OFFICERS OF THE BOSTON POLICE DEPARTMENT, THE IDENTITY AND NUMBER OF WHOM PRESENTLY UNKNOWN TO PLAINTIFFS Defendants	PLAINTIFF'S APPLICATION FOR A WRIT OF MANDAMUS

RELIEF SOUGHT

Plaintiff Laroy D. Cox applies pursuant to F.R.App.P. Rule 21(a) that this Court issue a Writ of Mandamus directed to the Honorable Judge Edward F. Harrington of the United States District Court for the District of Massachusetts ordering that he perform his legal duty to:

1. rule on the timeliness and legal sufficiency of Plaintiff's Motion for Recusal;

2. allow the Motion for Recusal and disqualify himself from hearing this Action; and

3. order that all motions decided by him after the filing of Plaintiff's Motion for Recusal be reconsidered by another Judge.

STATEMENT OF FACTS

This is a Civil Rights Action deriving from the Stuart Murder investigation of 1989 that was assigned to Justice Harrington's Courtroom in or about March, 1993. On 1 October 1993, Plaintiff filed a Motion for Recusal pursuant to 28 USC 144 and 28 USC 455 that is attached as Exhibit A, the subject of which was the Court's actions between September 8th and 30th, 1993. No Opposition were ever filed to that Motion. On October 8, 1993, without hearing, Justice Harrington denied the Motion. Exhibit B. His Decision made no ruling on the timeliness and legal sufficiency of the Motion's Affidavit but only denied it by calling it defamatory, by defending his actions that were the subject of the Motion, and by personally suggesting that if Plaintiff's Counsel does not like how he runs his Courtroom that she should withdraw from the Action. Exhibit B.

STATEMENT OF ISSUES PRESENTED

1. Does a Judge have a legal duty to first accept as true the alleged facts and then rule on the timeliness and legal sufficiency of an Affidavit in support of a Motion for Recusal and cannot deny the Motion based solely on his personal feelings that the alleged facts are false?
2. Must a Judge remove himself from a case if a timely filed Affidavit plus subsequent acts by the Court state sufficient facts showing personal bias and prejudice on the part of the Judge?
3. If a Judge fails to remove himself from an Action when

required to do so by his legal duty, are his rulings after such failure subject to reconsideration?

STATEMENT OF REASONS

"[T]he issue of judicial disqualification presents an extraordinary situation suitable for the exercise of our mandamus jurisdiction." In re United States, 666 F.2d 690, 694 (1st Cir. 1981). Mandamus is the appropriate remedy against a judge who refuses to recuse himself when required to do so by a statutory standard. E.g., Pepsico, Inc. v. McMillen, 764 F.2d 458 (7th Cir. 1985).

On the filing of an affidavit documenting personal bias or prejudice, the Court's inquiry is limited to determining whether the affidavit is both procedurally correct and legally sufficient to compel disqualification, and the Court may not pass on the truth of the matter alleged but must accept as true all factual assertions even when known by the Court to be false. Selfridge v. Gynecol Inc., 564 F.Supp. 57, 58 (D.Mass 1983) (emphasis added); e.g., Berger v. United States, 255 U.S. 22, 41 S.Ct. 230 (1921). A judge may not question either the truth of the allegations by affidavit made in support of a motion for recusal nor the good faith of the affidavit, even if the judge knows to a certainty that the allegations of personal prejudice are false. McCann v. Communications Design Corp, 775 F.Supp. 1506, 1523-24 (D.Conn. 1991); e.g., Berger, supra. If an affidavit of prejudice is legally sufficient, a Judge has no alternative but to recuse himself no matter how "defamatory" the Judge may consider the charges to be and even if they are known to the judge to be false. United States v. Hanrahan, 248 F.Supp. 471, 474 (D.DC 1965); e.g., Berger, supra.

Despite this clear law delineating Justice Harrington's legal duty regarding the subject Motion for Recusal, his Decision denying it made no ruling on its timeliness and legal sufficiency. Exhibit B. In fact, his Denial exhibited reasoning completely contrary to his legal duty as it is based on his deciding that the Affidavit's allegations were "false and insulting" and on his personal defense of his actions by suggesting that Plaintiff's Counsel should be the one to remove herself from the Action if she does not "appreciate" his Courtroom manner. Id. It should be noted that His Honor's Decision denied race and gender bias though no allegation of such was even stated in the Affidavit while it completely ignored the factual allegations of denial of due process and ex parte decisionmaking by him. Id.

The basis for Plaintiff's Motion for Recusal speaks for itself, is attached as Exhibit A, and Plaintiff respectfully refers the Court to it in order to avoid its duplication within the body of this Application. However, Plaintiff argues that Justice Harrington's Decision on the Motion is further support of the need for recusal. To require recusal, a charge of partiality must be supported by a factual basis that provides what "an objective, knowledgeable member of the public would find to be a reasonable basis for doubting the judge's impartiality." In re United States, supra, at 695.

In responding to Plaintiff Counsel's Affidavit alleging a factual basis for recusal, Justice Harrington not only without hearing openly ignored his legal duty of review but took it as an opportunity to personally attack Plaintiff's Counsel. Exhibit B. To any reasonable, objective observer of this Action, it would appear that because of some personal bias by Judge Harrington in this sensitive Civil Rights Action against "high ranking members of the Boston Police," he has decided that the Plaintiff is not entitled to the due process requirements of the Local Rules of the District Court, of the Federal Rules of Civil Procedure, nor the legal requirements of 28 USC 144 and 455. It appears that Plaintiff is especially not entitled to any equitable consideration warranting quashing of service of process instead of dismissal but that the "high ranking police" Defendants are entitled to be rewarded for ignoring Court Process for six months. Exhibit A at p. 7-8. It appears that this Action is solely an opportunity for his Honor to conduct his own personal method of probing into his personal conception of the truth or assumed "meritless" nature of Plaintiff's claims. Id and Exhibit B.

As all Decisions ruled upon by Justice Harrington after the filing of the improperly denied Motion for Recusal may be questioned for impartiality, such Decisions should be reconsidered by another Judge.

CONCLUSION

THEREFORE, Plaintiff asks that all of the above requested relief be allowed or any portion of it as deemed proper by the Court.

Plaintiff by his attorney,

Date:

Appendix E **Judicial Opinon, re: Liability of Prosecutior** - William G. Moore, Jr. v. Valder, et. al. (Appellate Decision)

[E]

United States Court of Appeals

FOR THE DISTRICT OF COLUMBIA CIRCUIT

Argued January 18, 1995 Decided September 22, 1995

Nos. 93-5341 and 93-5343

WILLIAM G. MOORE, JR.,
APPELLANT

v.

JOSEPH B. VALDER, *ET AL.*,
APPELLEES

On Appeal from the United States District Court
for the District of Columbia

(92cv02288 and 93cv00324)

Paul M. Pohl argued the cause for the appellant. On brief was *James E. Anklam.*

Robert V. Zener argued the cause for appellees Valder, *et al.*

Bills of costs must be filed within 14 days after entry of judgment. The court looks with disfavor upon motions to file bills of costs out of time.

Jonathan R. Siegel, Attorney, Department of Justice, argued the cause for appellee United States of America. On brief were *Frank W. Hunger*, Assistant Attorney General, *Eric H. Holder, Jr.*, United States Attorney, and *Barbara L. Herwig*, Attorney, Department of Justice. *Gordon W. Daiger* and *Robert M. Loeb* entered appearances.

Before: EDWARDS, *Chief Judge*; WALD and HENDERSON, *Circuit Judges*.

Opinion for the court filed by *Circuit Judge* HENDERSON.

KAREN LECRAFT HENDERSON, *Circuit Judge*: Appellant William G. Moore, Jr. (Moore) appeals the dismissal of his *Bivens* and Federal Tort Claims Act claims against Assistant United States Attorney Joseph B. Valder (Valder), six United States Postal Service Inspectors (postal inspectors) [1] and the United States. Moore sued for injuries allegedly caused by Valder's and the postal inspectors' malicious and retaliatory prosecution of him. We affirm in part and reverse in part.

I.

Moore was indicted in October 1988 on various counts of theft and fraud. Moore was chairman, president and chief executive officer of Recognition Equipment Incorporated (REI), a company interested in supplying the U.S. Postal Service (USPS) with address-scanning equipment. The indictment charged that Moore and Robert Reedy, another REI employee, engaged in a scheme to defraud the federal government by persuading William Spartin to recommend for the position of United States Postmaster General a candidate who favored using REI's address-scanning equipment. Spartin was both president of Gnau & Associates, Inc. (GAI), a consulting firm hired by REI, and president of a subsidiary of an executive search firm hired by the USPS to identify a qualified candidate to serve as Postmaster General. The indictment also accused Moore and Reedy of participating in

[1] The postal inspector defendants-appellees are Michael Hartman, Frank Korman, Robert Edwards, Pierce McIntosh, Daniel Harrington and Norman Robbins.

a scheme by which GAI employees paid money to Peter E. Voss, a member of the USPS Board of Governors, in return for Voss's steering business to GAI and its clients. REI had hired GAI at the suggestion of Voss. Five co-conspirators, including Voss and John R. Gnau, Jr., the principal of GAI, either pleaded guilty or testified about the fraud pursuant to a grant of immunity.

In November 1991, at the close of the government's case in Moore's criminal non-jury trial, the district court granted Moore's motion for a judgment of acquittal. *United States v. Recognition Equip. Inc.*, 725 F. Supp. 587 (D.D.C. 1989). The district court found insufficient evidence to support a reasonable inference that Moore and Reedy knew of either scheme. *Id.* Moore then filed a complaint in the U.S. District Court for the Northern District of Texas against Valder and the postal inspectors, asserting a *Bivens* [2] cause of action for malicious prosecution (malicious prosecution claim) and a *Bivens* claim for prosecution in retaliation for the exercise of his first amendment right (retaliatory prosecution claim).[3] Moore later filed a second complaint in the Northern District of Texas seeking recovery from the United States under the Federal Tort Claims Act (FTCA), 28 U.S.C. §§ 2671 *et seq.*, for the same alleged injuries.

In the two complaints Moore alleged that Valder and the postal inspectors maliciously prosecuted him, even though they knew that he was unaware of the fraud, based on his and REI's criticism of USPS procurement policies and on his recommendations to the President of qualified candidates for Postmaster General. In addition, Moore alleged other misconduct, including claims that Valder told several postal inspectors in the presence of a grand jury witness that he did

[2] *Bivens v. Six Unknown Named Agents of Fed. Bureau of Narcotics*, 403 U.S. 388 (1971) (recognizing a cause of action for damages against officials who violate constitutional or statutory rights under color of federal law).

[3] The complaint also asserted other constitutional and common-law tort claims which were dismissed by the district court. Moore does not appeal the dismissal of those claims.

not care whether Moore was in fact guilty because he wanted to secure a "high-profile" indictment to further his career; that Valder and the postal inspectors intimidated and coerced witnesses into changing their testimony to incriminate Moore; that they concealed evidence of Moore's innocence; that they manipulated witness testimony and presented to the grand jury false, incomplete and misleading written witness statements; that they lost, destroyed or concealed from the grand jury exculpatory information; that they disclosed grand jury testimony to third parties; and that Valder withheld material exculpatory information from Moore after indictment.

The district court dismissed the *Bivens* claims against Valder, holding that he was protected by absolute immunity. The court denied the postal inspectors' motion to dismiss the *Bivens* claims against them on the ground of qualified immunity and then transferred the remaining claims to the U.S. District Court for the District of Columbia, concluding that it lacked in personam jurisdiction. The FTCA complaint was also transferred and the parties stipulated to the consolidation of the two cases by the district court here.

The district court first denied Moore's motion to return the complaints to the Northern District of Texas. The court then dismissed the *Bivens* claims against the postal inspectors because Moore's complaint did not recite direct evidence of their alleged unconstitutional motive and therefore did not satisfy a heightened pleading standard. The court also dismissed the FTCA claims for lack of subject matter jurisdiction, holding that the alleged misconduct fell within the FTCA's discretionary function exception.

II.

On appeal Moore contends that Valder is not entitled to absolute immunity; that the court erred in applying a heightened pleading standard to his *Bivens* complaint; and that the FTCA's discretionary function exception does not preserve the United States's sovereign immunity from liability for the alleged misconduct. In analyzing his claims, we group the specific misconduct alleged by Moore into four categories:

pressuring witnesses into incriminating Moore; concealing and distorting exculpatory evidence to create misleading or incomplete witness accounts of what Moore knew about the alleged fraud;[4] withholding material exculpatory information from Moore after indictment; and disclosing grand jury testimony to unauthorized third parties.

A. *Claims Against Valder*

The district court dismissed Moore's *Bivens* claims against Valder, holding that Valder was protected by absolute immunity.[5] We review *de novo* a dismissal for failure to state a claim upon which relief can be granted but accept the facts as alleged in the complaint. *Kowal v. MCI Communications Corp.*, 16 F.3d 1271, 1276, 1273 (D.C. Cir. 1994). We hold that absolute immunity shields Valder from liability for the decision to prosecute Moore and for some, but not all, of the other alleged instances of misconduct.

In several decisions the Supreme Court has considered whether and to what extent a state or local prosecutor *qua* prosecutor is immune from liability under 28 U.S.C. § 1983. As the Court has recognized, the law of immunity in a *Bivens* claim against a federal official mirrors that in a section 1983 claim against a state official. *See, e.g., Butz v. Economou*, 438 U.S. 478, 504 (1978) (deeming it "untenable to draw a distinction for purposes of immunity law between suits

---

[4] We do not read Moore's complaint to allege that Valder or the postal inspectors *manufactured* false evidence to incriminate Moore. The complaint, construed favorably to Moore, alleges only that the written witness statements, prepared by Valder and the postal inspectors and submitted to the grand jury, created false impressions because they omitted important exculpatory testimony. Joint Appendix (JA) 377–78.

[5] According to the district court, "Valder was performing judicial and quasi-judicial functions. All of Valder's conduct relevant to this case was preparatory to presenting a case against Moore to the grand jury. The face of the complaint compels the conclusion that all of the acts attributed to Valder were prosecutorial functions...." JA 340.

brought against state officials under § 1983 and suits brought directly under the Constitution against federal officials"); *see also Briggs v. Goodwin*, 569 F.2d 10, 17–18 n.8 (D.C. Cir. 1977) ("*[A]ssuming* the rule of *Bivens* comprehends a damage action for a particular constitutional infringement by a federal officer, the federally-determined immunity applicable in such a case should be no different from the federally-determined immunity available in a § 1983 suit against a state official.") (emphasis original). Accordingly, we look to those decisions for guidance.

In *Imbler v. Pachtman*, 424 U.S. 409 (1976), the Supreme Court held that a prosecutor enjoys absolute immunity from section 1983 liability when he acts "as an advocate" by engaging in activities "intimately associated with the judicial phase of the criminal process." *Id.* at 430. As the Court in *Imbler* noted, the common law afforded absolute immunity to prosecutors for several reasons. Immunity encourages vigorous decisionmaking by reducing, if not eliminating, liability's inhibitory effect, *id.* at 424–25; it protects prosecutors against having "to answer in court each time [a defendant] charge[s] him with wrongdoing [which diverts] his energy and attention . . . from the pressing duty of enforcing the criminal law," *id.* at 425; and it ensures that judges are not influenced "by even the subconscious knowledge that a post-trial decision in favor of the accused might result in the prosecutor's being called upon to respond in damages for his error or mistaken judgment." *Id.* at 427. Alternative mechanisms, such as the trial judge's remedial powers, appellate review and post-conviction collateral remedies, exist to remedy injury caused by prosecutorial misconduct. *Id.* In addition, there are alternative ways to deter and punish prosecutorial misconduct, such as subjecting the prosecutor to criminal prosecution or professional discipline. *Id.* at 429.

The Court in *Imbler* held that "the same considerations of public policy that underlie the common-law rule likewise countenance absolute immunity under § 1983." *Id.* at 424. At a minimum, advocatory conduct includes "initiating a prosecution" and "presenting the State's case." *Id.* at 431.[6] Recognizing that "the duties of the prosecutor in his role as advocate for the State involve actions preliminary to the initiation of a prosecution and actions apart from the courtroom," the Court acknowledged that distinguishing between action taken as an advocate and action taken as an administrator or investigator "may present difficult questions." *Id.* at 431 n.33.

The line between advocatory conduct and administrative or investigative activity was refined in *Burns v. Reed*, 500 U.S. 478 (1991). Using a "functional approach," the Court emphasized that lower courts must look at the nature of the function performed, not the identity of the person performing it, to determine if a prosecutor is clothed with absolute immunity. The prosecutor must establish that the *conduct* under review was advocatory in nature. *Id.* at 486. The Court held that participation in a probable cause hearing ("appearing before a judge and presenting evidence in support of a motion for a search warrant") is protected by absolute immunity but giving legal advice to police officers is not. "Absolute immunity is designed to free the judicial process from the harassment and intimidation associated with litigation. That concern therefore justifies absolute prosecutorial immunity only for actions that are connected with the prosecutor's role in judicial proceedings, not for every litigation-inducing conduct." *Id.* at 494. The Court warned that "[a]lmost any action by a prosecutor, including his or her direct participation in purely investigative activity, could be said to be in some way related to the ultimate decision whether to prosecute, but we have never indicated that absolute immunity is that expansive." *Id.* at 495.

Most recently, the Court discussed the scope of absolute prosecutorial immunity in *Buckley v. Fitzsimmons*, 113 S. Ct.

[6] Additionally, "whether to present a case to a grand jury, whether to file an information, whether and when to prosecute, whether to dismiss an indictment against particular defendants, which witnesses to call, and what other evidence to present" are advocatory decisions. *Imbler*, 424 U.S. at 431 n.33.

2606 (1993). There, the Court reaffirmed that "as the function test of *Imbler* recognizes, the actions of a prosecutor are not absolutely immune merely because they are performed by a prosecutor." *Id.* at 2615. Advocatory conduct protected by absolute immunity "include[s] the professional evaluation of the evidence assembled by the police and appropriate preparation for its presentation at trial or before a grand jury after a decision to seek an indictment has been made." *Id.* But when a prosecutor "performs the investigative functions normally performed by a detective or police officer," he is entitled only to the qualified immunity that the detective or police officer enjoys. *Id.* at 2616–17.

In *Buckley,* the petitioner alleged that the prosecutors fabricated evidence during the preliminary investigation of a crime and made false statements at a press conference announcing the indictment of the petitioner. The Court held that the prosecutors did not have absolute immunity from liability for the alleged fabrication of evidence because they did not have probable cause to arrest or to initiate judicial proceedings. *Id.* at 2616. "Their mission at that time was entirely investigative in character. A prosecutor neither is, nor should consider himself to be, an advocate before he has probable cause to have anyone arrested." *Id.* The Court emphasized that the alleged fabrication occurred before a grand jury was convened and that when the grand jury eventually was convened, "its immediate purpose was to conduct a more thorough investigation of the crime—not to return an indictment against a suspect whom there was already probable cause to arrest." *Id.* The Court also held that a prosecutor is not absolutely immune from liability for making allegedly false statements to the press because statements to the media "have no functional tie to the judicial process." *Id.* at 2618.

Applying these holdings here, we conclude that Valder's prosecutorial immunity insulates him from liability for his unquestionably advocatory decision to prosecute Moore. His prosecutorial immunity also protects Valder from liability for allegedly concealing exculpatory evidence from the grand jury and for allegedly manipulating evidence before the grand jury to create a false impression of what Moore knew about the alleged fraudulent schemes. Valder's decisions regarding what evidence to put before the grand jury, and in what manner, are advocatory because they are central to the prosecutor's task of "initiating a prosecution" and "presenting the State's case." *Imbler*, 424 U.S. at 431; *see also Hill v. City of New York*, 45 F.3d 653, 661–62 (2nd Cir. 1995) (holding absolute immunity protects prosecutor from liability for withholding exculpatory evidence from grand jury). In addition, withholding after indictment information that is subject to disclosure under *Brady v. Maryland*, 373 U.S. 83 (1963), is advocatory. In *Imbler*, the prosecutor was alleged to have knowingly used false testimony and suppressed material exculpatory evidence at trial. The Court upheld the lower courts' rulings that the prosecutor was absolutely immune from potential liability for the alleged misconduct. As other courts have recognized, it follows from *Imbler* that the failure, be it knowing or inadvertent, to disclose material exculpatory evidence before trial also falls within the protection afforded by absolute prosecutorial immunity. *See Hill*, 45 F.3d at 662 (holding failure to turn over *Brady* material "after prosecutorial phase" of case had begun was covered by absolute prosecutorial immunity); *Carter v. Burch*, 34 F.3d 257, 262 (4th Cir. 1994) (holding absolute immunity protects prosecutor from liability for failing to give defense counsel materially exculpatory evidence).

Valder, however, has not met his burden of establishing that absolute immunity protects him from potential liability for the other instances of misconduct alleged by Moore. Intimidating and coercing witnesses into changing their testimony is not advocatory. It is rather a misuse of *investigative* techniques legitimately directed at exploring whether witness testimony is truthful and complete and whether the government has acquired all incriminating evidence. It therefore relates to a typical police function, the collection of information to be used in a prosecution. *See, e.g., Barbera v. Smith*, 836 F.2d 96, 100 (2d Cir. 1987) (holding "*acquiring* evidence which might be used in a prosecution," in contradistinction to "*organization, evaluation, and marshalling*" of such evidence, is activity of "police nature" and is therefore not entitled to absolute protection) (emphasis original). "When a prosecutor performs the investigative functions normally performed by a detective or police officer, it is 'neither appropriate nor justifiable that, for the same act, immunity should protect the one and not the other.'" *Buckley,* 113 S. Ct. at 2616 (quoting *Hampton v. Chicago,* 484 F.2d 602, 608 (7th Cir. 1973), *cert. denied,* 415 U.S. 917 (1974)).[7]

Finally, disclosing grand jury testimony to unauthorized third parties is not advocatory because it has no functional tie to the judicial process—it does not contribute to the government's case before a grand or petit jury. Like making statements at a press conference, unauthorized disclosure "does not involve the initiation of a prosecution, the presentation of the state's case in court, or actions preparatory for these functions." *Buckley,* 113 S. Ct. at 2618.[8]

B. *Claims Against the Postal Inspectors*

The district court dismissed Moore's claims against the postal inspectors because Moore's complaint did not allege direct evidence that they acted maliciously or in retaliation for constitutionally protected speech. Reviewing the dismissal *de novo* and taking the facts as alleged in Moore's com-

---

[7] And as the Supreme Court explained:

> A prosecutor may not shield his investigative work with the aegis of absolute immunity merely because, after a suspect is eventually arrested, indicted, and tried, that work may be retrospectively described as "preparation" for a possible trial.... When the functions of prosecutors and detectives are the same ... the immunity that protects them is also the same.

Buckley, 113 S. Ct. at 2617.

[8] While we conclude that absolute immunity does not protect Valder, he of course would be entitled to any qualified immunity available to the postal inspectors. Qualified immunity protects a government official who performs discretionary functions from liability for civil damages if he can show that his actions did not violate "clearly established statutory or constitutional rights of which a reasonable person would have known." *Harlow v. Fitzgerald,* 457 U.S. 800, 818 (1982).

plaint, *Kowal*, 16 F.3d at 1276, 1273, we affirm the dismissal of the malicious prosecution claim but hold that the district court erred in dismissing Moore's retaliatory prosecution claim.[9]

The district court did not address whether Moore's *Bivens* claims alleged the violation of clearly established law.[10] The court, therefore, "erred in deciding the heightened pleading issue before deciding the *threshold* 'essentially legal question whether the conduct of which the defendant complains violated clearly established law.'" *Kartseva v. Department of State*, 37 F.3d 1524, 1530 (D.C. Cir. 1994) (quoting *Siegert v. Gilley*, 500 U.S. 226 (1991) (emphasis original)). Further-

[9] As an initial matter, we reject Moore's argument that the district court here was precluded from reconsidering the Texas district judge's conclusion that Moore had "asserted a set of facts supporting each claim that, if found to be true regarding the element of malice, would overcome defendants' qualified immunity defense and entitle him to relief." JA 343–44. We first observe that the Texas district judge should not have ruled on the immunity issue because he found that he lacked personal jurisdiction over the postal inspectors. More importantly, we iterate that the district court below is bound to follow the law of *this* circuit. *See, e.g.*, 1B *Moore's Federal Practice* ("The district courts owe obedience, each to the court of appeals in its own circuit. It may happen, therefore, that a decision in the transferor court is in accordance with the view of the law as established by the court of appeals in its own circuit, but in the transferee circuit the law is either unsettled, or settled to the contrary.... If the issue has been settled ... the transferee court finds itself suspended between the doctrine of stare decisis and the doctrine of the law of the case. In such a circumstance the transferee court would invite reversal if it did not follow the decisions of its own court of appeals.").

[10] The parties appear to agree that prosecution in retaliation for speech protected by the first amendment violates a clearly established right. *See infra* note 12. Although the parties disputed whether the malicious prosecution claim survived the qualified immunity defense, the district court expressly found that it "need not address the question" because of its ruling that Moore's allegations were otherwise deficient. JA 355.

more, it has not been clearly established that malicious prosecution violates any constitutional or statutory right.[11] Accordingly, the postal inspectors' qualified immunity defeats Moore's malicious prosecution claim. *Harlow*, 457 U.S. at 818. Moore's *retaliatory* prosecution claim, however, does allege the violation of clearly established law.[12]

In publicly criticizing the USPS Moore unquestionably exercised his first amendment rights. Record evidence mani-

---

[11] *See Sami v. United States*, 617 F.2d 755, 773 (D.C. Cir. 1979) (citing with approval cases holding that "it takes more than a false arrest or malicious prosecution claim to rise to the dignity of a constitutional violation"); *see also McLaughlin v. Alban*, 775 F.2d 389, 392 (D.C. Cir. 1985) (concluding that plaintiff must "show not merely a mistaken prosecution or even a common law tort, but the violation of a constitutional right" to establish section 1983 claim); *Torres v. Superintendent of Police of Puerto Rico*, 893 F.2d 404, 409 (1st Cir. 1990) (holding section 1983 provides remedy only if plaintiff proves elements of malicious prosecution under state law and establishes that misuse of the legal proceedings was so egregious that he suffered deprivation of rights secured by fourteenth amendment) (citations omitted).

[12] *See, e.g., Haynesworth v. Miller*, 820 F.2d 1245, 1255–57 (D.C. Cir. 1987) (agreeing that "retaliatory prosecution [allegedly initiated solely because plaintiff refused to release civil claims of police misconduct against arresting officers] constitutes actionable First Amendment wrong"); *see also Norwell v. Cincinnati*, 414 U.S. 14, 16 (1973) (per curiam) (finding first amendment violation in retaliatory prosecution for "nonprovocatively voicing [ ] objection" to police conduct); *DeLoach v. Bevers*, 922 F.2d 618, 620 (10th Cir. 1990) ("An act taken in retaliation for the exercise of a constitutionally protected right is actionable under § 1983 even if the act, when taken for a different reason, would have been proper.") (quoting *Matzker v. Herr*, 748 F.2d 1142, 1150 (7th Cir. 1984)); *Magnotti v. Kuntz*, 918 F.2d 364, 368 (2d Cir. 1990) ("It is undisputed that retaliatory prosecution may expose a state official to section 1983 damages."); *Losch v. Parkesburg*, 736 F.2d 903, 907–08 (3d Cir. 1984) ("[I]nstitution of criminal action to penalize the exercise of one's First Amendment rights is a deprivation cognizable under § 1983.") (citing *Wilson v. Thompson*, 593 F.2d 1375, 1377 (5th Cir. 1979)).

fests that the criticism produced hostility in USPS management. Joint Appendix (JA) 154–156, 283. Two of the postal inspectors, who reported to USPS management, heard and did not repudiate Valder's declaration that Moore's innocence was irrelevant to the prosecution he intended to pursue. JA 32. These facts taken together constitute evidence sufficient to meet any applicable heightened pleading standard[13] and, accordingly, we remand Moore's retaliatory prosecution claim against the postal inspectors.

C. *Claims Against the United States*

The district court dismissed Moore's FTCA claims for lack of subject matter jurisdiction, holding that the alleged misconduct fell within the FTCA's "discretionary function" exception. We review the dismissal *de novo* but construe Moore's allegations in his favor. *Hohri v. United States,* 782 F.2d 227, 241 (D.C. Cir. 1986), *vacated on other grounds,* 482 U.S. 64 (1987).[14] We hold that only some of the alleged misconduct is covered by the exception.

The FTCA waives the sovereign immunity of the United States from suits for negligent or wrongful acts of government employees subject to certain exceptions. *See* 28 U.S.C. §§ 2671–2680. The "discretionary function" exception protects the federal government from liability for "[a]ny claim based upon . . . the exercise or performance or the failure to exercise or perform a discretionary function or duty on the part of a federal agency or an employee of the Government, whether or not the discretion involved be abused." 28 U.S.C. § 2680(a). The exception "preserves the preexisting cloak of governmental immunity for some category of activities."

[13] In *Kartseva v. Department of State,* 37 F.3d 1524, 1530–31 (D.C. Cir. 1994), we explained this circuit's two-level heightened pleading standard.

[14] Because we accept Moore's version of the facts, we reject his argument that the district court should not have decided whether the discretionary function exception applied without permitting Moore an opportunity to conduct discovery and develop a "concrete record."

Gray v. Bell, 712 F.2d 490, 508 (D.C. Cir. 1983), *cert. denied*, 465 U.S. 1100 (1984). We "must examine carefully the allegations made to determine whether they are sufficiently separable from protected discretionary decisions. If such separability exists, then the conduct of the prosecutor may be actionable under the FTCA." *Id.* at 515. But where the "allegation of improper investigatory conduct is inextricably tied to the decision to prosecute and the presentation of evidence to the Grand Jury," the discretionary function applies and preserves governmental immunity. *Id.* at 516.

Deciding whether to prosecute, assessing a witness's credibility to ensure that he is giving an accurate and complete account of what he knows, identifying the evidence to submit to the grand jury and determining whether information is "exculpatory" and "material" and therefore must be disclosed pursuant to a *Brady* request [15] are actions that require the prosecutor to exercise his professional judgment. They are therefore quintessentially discretionary.[16] Accordingly, the United States enjoys immunity from Moore's claims that Valder and the postal inspectors pressured witnesses into incriminating him, concealed and distorted exculpatory evidence to create a false impression of what he knew about the

---

[15] We recognize that internal regulations of the Department of Justice direct that "when a prosecutor conducting a grand jury inquiry is personally aware of substantial evidence which directly negates the guilt of a subject of the investigation, the prosecutor must present or otherwise disclose such evidence to the grand jury before seeking an indictment against such a person." Department of Justice Manual, 9-11.233 (October 1, 1990). Putting aside the question whether this regulation creates any enforceable right, we note that deciding what this regulation requires under a specific set of circumstances is itself a discretionary act.

[16] We are guided by our decision in *Gray* where we held that allegations that the defendants "deliberately present[ed] false and misleading evidence to and with[held] exculpatory evidence from the Grand Jury" are within the discretionary function exception because they are "insufficiently separable from the discretionary decision to initiate prosecution." 712 F.2d at 495, 516.

fraud schemes and withheld material exculpatory information from him after the grand jury returned an indictment.

Disclosing grand jury testimony to unauthorized third parties, however, is *not* a discretionary activity nor is it inextricably tied to matters requiring the exercise of discretion. Rather, it is a discrete activity, sufficiently separable from protected discretionary decisions to make the discretionary function exception inapplicable to this allegation. We express no view whether the allegation is otherwise cognizable under the FTCA or whether it is supported by the evidence.

We therefore affirm in part, reverse in part and remand to the district court for proceedings consistent with this opinion.

So ordered.

Appendix F **Civil Rights Complaint, Prosecutorial Misconduct** - William G. Moore, Jr. v. Joseph B Valder, et. al.

ORIGINAL

[F]

IN THE UNITED STATES DISTRICT COURT
FOR THE NORTHERN DISTRICT OF TEXAS
DALLAS DIVISION

WILLIAM G. MOORE, JR. and BLANCHE K. MOORE,

Plaintiffs,

v.

JOSEPH B. VALDER, MICHAEL HARTMAN, FRANK KORMAN, ROBERT EDWARDS, PIERCE McINTOSH, DANIEL HARRINGTON, (FIRST NAME UNKNOWN) ROBBINS, and OTHERS as of yet unknown, hereby designated as John Doe defendants 1-25,

Defendants.

Civil Action No. 3-91 CV2491-G

ORIGINAL COMPLAINT

I. JURISDICTION AND VENUE

1. The jurisdiction of this Court is invoked under Title 28 U.S.C. §§ 1331 and 1367(a). This suit is authorized by the First, Fourth and Fifth Amendments of the Constitution of the United States and such other State and Federal laws as may be applicable. Venue in this action is properly situated in the United States District Court for the Northern District of Texas, pursuant to 28 U.S.C. §§ 1391(b) and (e). Plaintiffs seek damages in excess of $50,000 for injuries sustained by them which were caused by the actions of the defendants.

II. PARTIES

2. Plaintiff William G. Moore, Jr. is a citizen of the United States who resides in Dallas, Texas. Plaintiff is the former Chairman, President and Chief Executive Officer of Recognition Equipment Incorporated ("REI").

3. Plaintiff Blanche K. ("Chelen") Moore is the wife of Plaintiff William G. Moore, Jr. and resides with him in Dallas, Texas.

4. Defendants are employees of the United States Government and its agencies, including the United States Department of Justice and the United States Postal Service ("USPS"), who, acting in their ministerial and individual capacities, did conspire to interfere with and violate, and did interfere with and violate, plaintiffs' rights and privileges, and did deprive Plaintiff William G. Moore, Jr. of his liberty and both plaintiffs of their property without due process of law, in conflict with the laws and Constitution of the United States and the laws of the State of Texas and the District of Columbia, as more fully appears herein below. Such defendants include:

a. Defendant Joseph Valder, who was at all relevant times an Assistant U.S. Attorney for the District of Columbia. Said defendant was responsible for the investigation and the overseeing of the Grand

Jury investigation which culminated in the wrongful indictment of Plaintiff William G. Moore, Jr. Defendant Valder, acting individually and/or in concert with the other defendants, also was responsible for the pre-trial activities and trial of the case against Plaintiff William G. Moore, Jr. Said defendant is sued in his individual capacity.

b. Defendants Frank Korman, Michael Hartman, Robert Edwards, Pierce McIntosh, Daniel Harrington (first name unknown) Robbins, and Postal Inspectors and other employees of the USPS who are presently unknown to plaintiffs (and hereinafter are referred to as "John Doe defendants 1-25"), and who were at all relevant times Postal Inspectors of the United States Postal Inspection Service or otherwise employed by the USPS. Defendants Korman and Hartman oversaw the investigation and were involved at all relevant stages. Each defendant Postal Inspector is sued in his own individual capacity. All of the defendant Postal Inspectors, whether known or unknown, shall be referred to collectively as "Postal Inspectors."

III. NATURE OF THIS CASE

5. The incidents on which plaintiffs' lawsuit is based occurred as a result of malicious, deliberate,

intentional, reckless and negligent misconduct by Assistant United States Attorney Joseph Valder and the U.S. Postal Inspection Service and its agents, as named and/or described above, before, during, and after a Grand Jury investigation which culminated in an indictment being returned against Plaintiff William G. Moore, Jr., REI, and another employee of REI on October 6, 1988 in Washington, D.C. All defendants in the indictment were acquitted of all charges by United States District Judge George Revercomb on November 20, 1989. It became apparent that the investigation, Grand Jury proceedings and handling of the post-indictment proceedings by the defendants were punctuated by gross violations and abuses of plaintiffs' rights as detailed below.

6. This action is brought to seek fair compensation for the catastrophic financial injury, humiliation, mental suffering and anguish inflicted upon plaintiffs as a result of the wrongful acts of defendants. This action is also filed to ensure that these defendants and others are deterred from engaging in such wrongful activity again.

IV. FACTS

7. Plaintiff William G. Moore, Jr. is the former Chairman, Chief Executive Officer and President of REI. He is a graduate of Georgetown University and has served on its Board of Regents. He served in the U.S. Army, obtaining the rank of

Captain, and saw service in Vietnam. REI was a manufacturer of, among other products, optical character recognition ("OCR") systems. The Company was at all relevant times headquartered in Irving, Texas. At the time Moore joined REI in 1982, the company, which had suffered losses for five years, had lost $14.2 million in the preceding year and was on the verge of bankruptcy. Within one year, Moore had turned REI around, and REI reported net income of $9.5 million. By 1986, REI had reached $241.8 million in revenues, and it was considered one of the most dynamic and successful publicly-held corporations in the Dallas area. Because of his success, Moore was the recipient of various significant honors from organizations across the country, including being named Dallas Business Man of the Year. He served as Chairman of the American Electronics Association and on the Boards of various civic and charitable organizations.

8. REI had developed multi-line optical character reading ("MLOCR") equipment which would automatically read several lines of an address to code and assign a nine-digit zip code to a piece of mail. REI desired to sell the product to USPS. REI believed it would speed up the mail system and save USPS millions of dollars per year.

9. At the time relevant to the charges in the indictment, USPS was employing single-line OCR equipment which

could only read the bottom line of an address, and the efficiency of single-line technology was dependent upon the public use of the nine-digit zip code. The single-line OCR technology was not successful because the public use of the nine-digit zip code did not meet USPS' expectations. Since the indictment, USPS has converted its automated sorting equipment to multi-line technology.

10. At the time of Moore's arrival at REI, there had been a longstanding conflict between REI and various senior managers within USPS. In late 1983, then Postmaster General William Bolger announced that there would be no future for multi-line technology in the automation plans of USPS. One high-ranking postal manager stated that REI would never receive any multi-line production awards as long as he was with USPS.

11. After the single-line decision by USPS, Plaintiff William G. Moore, Jr. informed Postmaster General Bolger that single-line technology was an unsound strategy, and that Moore intended to go directly to USPS Board of Governors, the media, and the United States Congress to try and stop the ineffective and wasteful single-line implementation. Moore did, in fact, -- as he was Constitutionally permitted to do -- communicate about the subject with various Congressmen and Senators, including Texas Congressmen Jack Brooks and the late Mickey Leland, Missouri Congressman Richard Gephardt and Alaska

Senator Ted Stevens. As previously noted, USPS now uses the multi-line approach advocated by REI.

12. In the course of REI's efforts to obtain contracts from USPS, which was supposed to review in an open, fair and impartial manner all competing technologies for mail scanning and sorting equipment, REI hired the consulting firm of Gnau and Associates, Inc. ("GAI"). John Gnau was a principal of GAI. The use of this consulting firm had been suggested to REI by a a member of the USPS Board of Governors.

13. In early 1985, the U.S. Postal Inspection Service began an investigation into possible illegal payments from Gnau to Peter E. Voss, then a member of the USPS Board of Governors. It was later determined that a conspiracy in which Gnau made illegal payments to Voss existed between Voss, John Gnau, Michael Marcus (the Treasurer of GAI) and William Spartin (President of GAI). Voss, Gnau and Marcus pled guilty to criminal charges. Spartin and Sharon Peterson, an administrative assistant to Voss, agreed to cooperate in exchange for immunity from prosecution. Frank Bray, REI's Vice President of Distributor Sales, also received immunity.

14. During the investigation, Defendant Valder and the Postal Inspectors, including at least Defendants Hartman and Korman as well as various other unknown defendants, desperately tried to find a way to link William G. Moore, Jr.,

to the conspiracy. However, the evidence clearly and unequivocally demonstrated that Moore knew absolutely nothing about the conspiracy. None of the thousands of documents subpoenaed by the Grand Jury during the investigation indicated that Moore, or for that matter REI, had knowledge of the conspiracy and related unlawful activities. Moore repeatedly informed the Postal Inspectors and AUSA Valder that he had no knowledge of the conspiracy. None of the five admitted conspirators - Voss, Gnau, Marcus, Peterson and Spartin - gave any testimony even remotely indicating that Moore knew of, or participated in, the conspiracy. In fact, several conspirators testified at trial that they actively tried to disguise the conspiracy from Moore and had previously told that to Valder and certain of the other defendants.

15. The obvious issue in any criminal action against Moore would be whether he had knowledge of and participated in the conspiracy or the unlawful acts of the consultants and Voss. The evidence gathered in the massive investigation showed clearly and without exception that Moore had no knowledge of the conspiracy or the unlawful acts. The Postal Inspectors and AUSA Valder knew that such lack of knowledge would prevent the return of any proper indictment against Moore. Notwithstanding the above, Defendants Valder, Hartman, Korman, Edwards, McIntosh, Harrington, Robbins, and the John

Doe defendants who are presently unknown to plaintiffs, deliberately, systematically and without regard to Moore's Constitutional right to fair investigation and fair consideration by the Grand Jury, concealed from the Grand Jury crucial and extensive exculpatory testimony from the co-conspirators (Gnau, Peterson, Marcus, Spartin and Voss) that Moore was not told about, and did not know about, the unlawful scheme to pay kickbacks to Voss.

16. Defendants engaged in unusual, unlawful and unconstitutional investigative techniques to intimidate and coerce witnesses to try to implicate Moore and to control the flow of information to the Grand Jury in order to mislead the Grand Jury to return an indictment when none was warranted. These activities were done in clear disregard of the defendants' obligations as employees of the United States; these activities were done by defendants with malice and in clear violation of Moore's right to a fair investigation; these activities were done by defendants in an attempt to obtain publicity for themselves and seek career advancement; and these unlawful activities were done by defendants in an attempt to "punish" Moore for exercising his constitutionally-protected rights to criticize USPS procurement decisions.

17. By concealing and distorting the evidence as they did, AUSA Valder and the Postal Inspectors acted outside their

discretion, violated their employer's policies and procedures, and knowingly violated plaintiffs' clearly established Constitutional rights. The methods designed by the defendants to withhold key exculpatory evidence and to manufacture false and misleading testimony are detailed below.

18. AUSA Valder and the Postal Inspectors drafted and used written "witness statements" to shape the evidence presented to the Grand Jury. These misleading "witness statements" were false, inaccurate, incomplete and misleading and were presented to the Grand Jury even though live witnesses were available to testify. Even though all the witnesses told AUSA Valder and the Postal Inspectors that Moore was unaware of the conspiracy, not one single witness statement written by the Postal Inspectors included this crucial, exculpatory statement. Additionally, AUSA Valder and the Postal Inspectors refused to allow witnesses to amend these statements, even though it was supposedly the witnesses', not the Postal Inspectors', statements. These statements were thereafter presented to the Grand Jury as the witnesses' own statements. For example, Frank Bray was interviewed several times in an intimidating fashion by the Postal Inspectors, including Inspectors Edwards and Harrington, in an attempt to have him change his testimony that Moore was unaware of the conspiracy. Incredibly, AUSA Valder and the Postal Inspectors refused to

allow Bray to include in "his" statement that, to his knowledge, REI and Moore were not aware of the payoffs. Bray and his attorney, Ellen Huvelle (now a Judge on the Superior Court of the District of Columbia) amended their version of Bray's statement to include such language, but the Postal Inspectors refused to change it. Moreover, Bray and Ms. Huvelle were not permitted to take the amended version of Bray's statement with them after their meeting with the Postal Inspectors, and the amended version mysteriously disappeared by the time of trial. The Grand Jury was thereafter read the statement written by the Postal Inspectors, which purported to be Bray's statement, without the exculpatory statement. Additionally, AUSA Valder promised Bray and Ms. Huvelle that he would ask Bray the key questions about Moore's knowledge in the Grand Jury, but Valder thereafter refused to do so.

19. John Gnau and Peter Voss were the two leaders of the conspiracy. Gnau repeatedly told the Postal Inspectors that he never told Moore about his illicit relationship with Voss. However, "his" statement written by the Postal Inspectors deliberately omitted this fact. Voss, who was serving a prison sentence on these charges and was clearly available to the Government, was never called by the Government to testify at trial.

20. Despite the fact that Postal Inspectors are trained to take detailed notes, virtually none of the notes taken by Postal Inspectors during their interviews of various witnesses contained the witnesses' crucial statements to the effect that Moore was not told of the conspiracy. These key statements were deliberately omitted by the Postal Inspectors in order to avoid their responsibility to conduct a fair investigation and to preserve exculpatory material.

21. AUSA Valder and the Postal Inspectors threatened and intimidated William Spartin in an attempt to coerce incriminating testimony from him after he repeatedly told the Government that to his knowledge, Moore did not know of the payoffs to Voss. Such tactics included a pre-planned tearing-up of Spartin's immunity letter in front of him and threats to prosecute Spartin's son. This was despite the fact that a lie detector test had indicated that Spartin was being truthful when he said Moore and REI were not informed of the conspiracy. Moreover, unbeknownst to Spartin, the lie detector test was conducted by Inspector Robbins, who repeatedly tried to trick and coerce Spartin into giving incriminating testimony against Moore.

22. AUSA Valder and the Postal Inspectors, including Inspector McIntosh, violated Federal Rule of Criminal Procedure 6(e)(2), which protects the secrecy of Grand Jury proceedings,

by giving Spartin and former Postmaster General Paul Carlin access to the Grand Jury testimony of other witnesses for the purpose of influencing Spartin's testimony and for the apparent purpose of assisting Carlin, a private plaintiff, to pursue civil litigation in connection with his dismissal from the Postal Service. The Postal Inspectors even gave Carlin a copy of a draft indictment for his review.

23. AUSA Valder deliberately withheld Brady v. Maryland exculpatory material from attorneys for Moore and REI before and during their trial, despite a Court Order to turn over even "borderline" Brady material. Such Brady material included the results of lie detector tests in which Mr. Spartin made 19 references to Moore's and REI's lack of knowledge as to the conspiracy, and the amended version of Frank Bray's statement in which he added a paragraph that to his knowledge, Moore and REI were unaware of the payoffs. If this material had been turned over to the defense as it should have been, Moore would likely have been spared the expense and humiliation of a long, extensively publicized trial.

24. Through the use of the above malicious, improper and unconstitutional tactics, AUSA Valder and the defendant Postal Inspectors were able to obtain an indictment against William G. Moore, Jr. However, nowhere in the 46-page conspiracy charge -- nowhere in its 10 objects, 58 means and

methods or 96 overt acts -- did the charge allege that Moore or REI even know that GAI was paying bribes to Voss, much less that they agreed to these payments. This deliberate attempt to hide the only real issue in the indictment by pure volume and verbosity was not successful. Following the Government's presentation of its case at trial, Judge George Revercomb acquitted Moore and all other defendants.

25. After the indictment, REI was debarred from all postal procurements. The United States forced REI to place Moore on leave of absence and to sever him from any management involvement with REI. As a result of the indictment, the Company began to flounder and the stock price plunged. The company was eventually the subject of a takeover attempt, had a change of control and Plaintiff William G. Moore, Jr. lost his job. The wrongful investigation/indictment and prosecution prevented REI from bidding, and in all probability winning, hundreds of millions of dollars in postal automation contracts. The wrongful investigation/indictment caused the plaintiffs to sustain severe financial injury.

26. Following the indictment, Plaintiff William G. Moore, Jr. was subjected to the various aspects of criminal justice system processing, including arraignment and fingerprinting. He was processed not once, but twice; one time by the Postal Inspectors, and the second time by the District

of Columbia police. He was briefly jailed in the District of Columbia during this processing.

27. There was a tremendous amount of media publicity during the unlawful investigation, following the indictment and during the trial, all of which caused plaintiffs humiliation, physical and mental suffering and anguish, and which required medical treatment for both plaintiffs.

28. The indictment named as part of the overt acts of the conspiracy such Constitutionally protected actions as the plaintiffs' lobbying of Congress for changes to the mail system. The defendants also sought to prosecute Plaintiff William G. Moore, Jr. for suggesting qualified candidates for the position of Postmaster General, even though he had been requested to do so by the White House and was Constitutionally entitled to do so.

29. As a result of the above-described unlawful activity and violations of plaintiffs' Constitutional rights, plaintiffs suffered and continue to suffer great financial losses, humiliation, embarrassment, physical and mental suffering, as well as loss of reputation in and among business associates, friends, and family.

30. As a result of the above-described unlawful activity and violations of plaintiffs' Constitutional rights, including voluminous unreasonable requests for personal and

business documents, including tax returns and bank records, and alleged surveillance and possibly wiretaps, defendants did invade the privacy of the plaintiffs and cause them injury.

31. AUSA Valder and the Postal Inspectors are not entitled to official immunity for the following reasons:

a. The actions of AUSA Valder and the Postal Inspectors and the John Doe defendants violated clearly established Constitutional rights which a reasonable person would have known and recognized.

b. AUSA Valder and the Postal Inspectors and the John Doe defendants took the described actions with the malicious intention to cause injury to plaintiff and to cause deprivation of plaintiffs' constitutional rights.

c. AUSA Valder and the Postal Inspectors had no discretion to act as they did since they violated, ignored and otherwise failed to comply with regulations and policies designed to guide their actions. The investigative tactics used were so extreme that no reasonable person would accept them as fair and lawful.

d. The Postal Inspectors undertook certain unlawful and improper actions on their own accord without direction from their supervisors or the United

States Attorney's Office, including the disclosure of secret Grand Jury material to witnesses, as stated in the United States Department of Justice Office of Professional Responsibility's letter dated May 30, 1991.

e. AUSA Valder acted in an investigative capacity during the course of the investigation, thereby losing his objectivity and violating his duty to fairly uphold the laws of the United States.

f. AUSA Valder acted in a non-advocatory role during the investigation, especially when he withheld, and failed to preserve, exculpatory evidence.

g. AUSA Valder continually provided inaccurate and misleading legal advice to the Postal Inspectors investigating the case.

FIRST CAUSE OF ACTION

32. By the aforesaid withholding of exculpatory evidence and by the presentation of false and misleading evidence to the Grand Jury, the defendants deprived the plaintiffs of their rights to due process and to an informed, fair and impartial Grand Jury as guaranteed by the Fifth Amendment of the United States Constitution.

SECOND CAUSE OF ACTION

33. The aforesaid actions of defendants constituted a slander and defamation of Plaintiff William G. Moore, Jr. The actions taken also constituted an unlawful invasion of plaintiffs' privacy, false arrest and abuse of process and malicious prosecution, all in violation of the laws of the State of Texas and of the District of Columbia, which this Court may adjudicate as pendant to the other four causes of action.

THIRD CAUSE OF ACTION

34. By the aforesaid improper and malicious activities, the defendants deprived the plaintiffs of their property without due process of law as guaranteed by the Fifth Amendment to the United States Constitution.

FOURTH CAUSE OF ACTION

35. By the aforesaid improper and malicious activities, the defendants deprived the plaintiffs of their rights to be free from unreasonable seizures as guaranteed by the Fourth Amendment of the United States Constitution, in that Plaintiff William G. Moore, Jr. was seized as he awaited processing, and furthermore, plaintiffs were forced to post bond and attend a trial based upon the improperly obtained indictment.

FIFTH CAUSE OF ACTION

36. By the aforesaid improper and malicious activities, which caused plaintiffs to deplete financial and human resources, the defendants attempted to punish Plaintiff William G. Moore, Jr. because he directed criticism against the USPS, thereby depriving the Plaintiffs of their rights to free expression and to petition the government for redress of grievances guaranteed by the First Amendment of the United States Constitution.

DAMAGES

37. As a result of the investigation and indictment, REI stock, of which Plaintiff William G. Moore, Jr. owned more than 100,000 shares, dropped from about $22 per share to about $5 per share. A change of control at REI occurred during the trial which would not have taken place if there had not been an indictment. As a result, Plaintiff William G. Moore, Jr. lost his job and suffered extensive financial injury.

38. In the three years prior to the indictment, Plaintiff William G. Moore, Jr.'s average compensation was more than $1 million per year. After the indictment, the value of Moore's stock ownership declined from $2 million to $500,000. Plaintiff William G. Moore, Jr.'s stock options decreased in value by at least another $2 million, and his annual income was, and has been, greatly reduced.

39. As further result of the indictment, Plaintiff William G. Moore, Jr. has been unable to find a position comparable to his previous employment. Plaintiff's reputation has been damaged, and he has been forced to resign from a number of boards and appointments.

40. The ordeal of investigation, indictment and trial has exacted a terrible physical and emotional toll on plaintiffs. Shortly after being notified of the impending indictment in late summer of 1988, Plaintiff William G. Moore, Jr. was treated at the emergency room at Parkland Hospital in Dallas for symptoms which were subsequently diagnosed as an acute stress reaction. Since the investigation began, Plaintiff Blanche Moore has suffered from chronic insomnia combined with Temporomandibular joint disorder (often called TMJ). She is currently under physician's care for chronic neck, back and leg pains.

41. WHEREFORE, Plaintiffs request this Court to assess compensatory damages against each defendant, jointly and severally, in at least the following amounts, and which amounts will be proven in detail at trial of this action:

(a) Lost Earnings - $17 million;

(b) Decrease in value of stock and stock options - $5 million;

(c) Personal suffering, humiliation and emotional distress - $10 million; and

(d) An amount adequate to compensate Mr. Moore for defense costs incurred during the investigation and trial.

42. In order to deter defendants and others from engaging in such unlawful and unconstitutional activities, Plaintiffs further request punitive damages against each defendant, plus costs and attorneys' fees, and any other and further relief as the Court may deem just and equitable.

DEMAND FOR JURY TRIAL

43. Plaintiffs hereby demand a trial by jury of all issues so triable in this cause of action.

Respectfully submitted,

JONES, DAY, REAVIS & POGUE

Jean M. Perron

Jean M. Perron
Texas State Bar No. 14085400
2300 Trammell Crow Center
2001 Ross Avenue
Dallas, Texas 75201
(214) 220-3939
(214) 969-5100 (Facsimile)

Attorneys for Plaintiffs

Of Counsel:

Paul Michael Pohl
Pennsylvania State Bar No. 21625
Edward C. Schmidt
Pennsylvania State Bar No. 16356
John J. Mead
Pennsylvania State Bar No. 39610

JONES, DAY, REAVIS & POGUE
One Mellon Bank Center
500 Grant Street, 31st Floor
Pittsburgh, PA 15219
(412) 391-3939
(412) 394-7959 (Facsimile)

Dated: November 19, 1991

4692g

Appendix G Domestic Relations, Child Custody - Interrogatories

[G]

COMMONWEALTH OF MASSACHUSETTS

SUFFOLK, ss

PROBATE AND FAMILY COURT
DOCKET NO. ▬▬▬▬

▬▬▬▬, Plaintiff

vs.

▬▬▬▬, Defendant

FIRST SET OF INTERROGATORIES PROPOUNDED BY THE DEFENDANT ▬▬▬▬ TO BE ANSWERED BY THE PLAINTIFF ▬▬▬▬

The Defendant in the above-entitled matter, ▬▬▬▬ submits interrogatories to be answered by the Plaintiff, ▬▬▬▬ pursuant to Mass. R. Dom. R.P. 33.

DEFINITIONS AND INSTRUCTIONS

1. The term "communication" includes, but is not limited to letters, telegrams, telexes, inter-or intra-office memoranda or communications, envelopes, and all other written or oral communications of whatever form, notes and memoranda of meetings or oral communications and sound recordings and transcripts thereof.

2. The term "financial records" includes, but is not limited to bankbook and statements, purchase orders, canceled checks, check stubs, invoices, bills, order forms, receipts, debit and credit memoranda, applications, accounts, certificates of condition, books of account (including journals, ledgers and the like) and financial statements.

3. The term "business records" includes, but is not limited to, minutes whether formal or informal or directors' stockholders', partners' or trustees' meetings, stock transfer records,

8. The term "property" whether identifying real or personal, tangible or intangible, shall include property inside or outside the United States of America.

9. The words "you" or "yours" mean the Plaintiff, and each of his present and former agents, employers, and all other persons acting or purporting to act on behalf of the Plaintiff William Bulger, Jr., but the use of such terms shall not be construed so as to limit the information provided to that which is within the personal knowledge of such party.

10. In answering each interrogatory, you will make such inquiry of your agents, servants, and attorneys and examine all bills, letters, financial statements, records, books of account, canceled checks and any other documents which in any way concern the matters dealt with by these interrogatories.

11. If you cannot answer an interrogatory, with exactness, you will answer to the best of your ability. If you are unable to answer the interrogatory, you will set forth in detail your reason for being unable to answer.

INTERROGATORY NO. 1

If you are presently employed, state your work days and hours and whether you are required to put in overtime.

INTERROGATORY NO. 2

On average, what proportion of each day do you spend with the parties' minor child, Monica ?

INTERROGATORY NO. 3

State with specificity how you provide for Monica's care when you are not available, naming each person and/or institution that has been engaged for this purpose.

INTERROGATORY NO. 4

List all income received by you or advanced on your behalf since **January 2004**, including but not limited to the nature, source and amount of all income.

INTERROGATORY NO. 5

Describe your current state of health and list the name, address and telephone number of each physician, medical clinic, or nurse practitioner you have consulted for yourself during the last 24 months, and with respect to each consultation, state the date, purpose, diagnosis, and treatment.

INTERROGATORY NO. 6

State whether you are currently taking any medication and list each medication, the dates on which you have taken it, and its purpose.

INTERROGATORY NO. 7

Fully describe your plans for the minor child's educational development and how you intend to implement such plans.

INTERROGATORY NO. 8

Fully describe your plans for the minor child's religious education and development and how you intend to implement such plans.

INTERROGATORY NO. 9

Describe your plans for the minor child's extracurricular activities and how you intend to implement such plans.

INTERROGATORY NO. 10

Describe with specificity why you feel you would be better custodian than the Defendant ▬▬▬ ▬▬▬.

INTERROGATORY NO. 11

State with specificity your greatest strengths and weaknesses as a parent. Include discussion of all physical and emotional disorders you have been treated for.

INTERROGATORY NO. 12

State with specificity the Defendant ▬▬▬ ▬▬▬ greatest strengths and weaknesses as a parent.

INTERROGATORY NO. 13

Describe how you discipline ▬▬▬

INTERROGATORY NO. 14

State any difficulties which ▬▬▬ may be experiencing and how you are equipped to deal with these difficulties.

INTERROGATORY NO. 15

Describe in detail the nature, extent and dates of all communications which you have had with any member of the Defendant's family since ▬▬▬ 2007, including but not limited to the individual with whom you communicated and whether you initiated the communication.

INTERROGATORY NO. 16

Do you plan to relocate from your present residence? If so, describe your relocation plans.

INTERROGATORY NO. 17

Describe with specificity each attempt you made to develop and/or foster a relationship between the Defendant and ▬▬▬ from January 29, 2007 to the present time.

INTERROGATORY NO. 18

List the name, address, and telephone number of each person who has knowledge of relevant facts concerning the issues of custody and visitation involved in this case, and for each such person state the nature of the knowledge.

INTERROGATORY NO. 19

List each person you may or will call as a witness in the trial of this matter. With respect to each, list name, address, telephone number, and issues concerning the anticipated testimony.

INTERROGATORY NO. 20

Fully describe the origin of the funds advanced by you to finance this litigation, including but not limited to legal fees and costs.

▬▬▬▬▬▬
by her attorney,

____
David C. Grossack, Esquire
1320 Centre Street, Suite 103
Newton, MA 02134
BBO # 212890

Dated: ▬▬▬▬ 30, 2007

Appendix H Appendix H **Civil Rights Complaint** - Shirley Barron v. Internal Revenue Service Special Agent, et. al.

[H]

UNITED STATES DISTRICT COURT
FOR THE DISTRICT OF NEW HAMPSHIRE

Shirley Barron and Shirley Barron, in her capacity as Administratrix of The Estate of Bruce Barron, Esquire	*	**AMENDED COMPLAINT AND JURY DEMAND** Civil Action No. 97-271-JD
v.	*	
United States of America (Department of Treasury, Internal Revenue Service)	*	
and	*	
Donna Greeley, Revenue Officer of the Internal Revenue Service	*	

NOW COMES Shirley Barron, an individual and Shirley Barron, in her capacity as the Administratrix of The Estate of Bruce E. Barron, Esquire and complains against the United States of America, acting through the Department of Treasury, Internal Revenue Service, and against Donna Greeley, present and/or former Revenue Officer of the Internal Revenue Service, as follows:

STATEMENT OF THE CASE

This is a lawsuit brought against the United States of America, acting through the Department of Treasury, Internal Revenue Service and against one Donna Greeley, present or formerly the Revenue Officer of the Internal Revenue Service, by Shirley Barron, individually and in her capacity as Administratrix of the Estate of Bruce Barron, Esquire. Commencing in approximately 1993, the Internal Revenue Service commenced a collection proceeding against the deceased, Bruce E. Barron, Esquire, and, by virtue of their joint tax return, against his wife and widow, Plaintiff Shirley

BRENNAN, CARON, LENEHAN & IACOPINO
85 BROOK STREET, MANCHESTER, NEW HAMPSHIRE 03104
603-668-8300

Barron. The Internal Revenue Service has established regulations and procedures which it is required to follow in any such collection proceeding. From 1993 to 1996, the Internal Revenue Service, agents and employees of the Internal Revenue Service, and Revenue Officer Greeley dissected every portion of the lives of Bruce E. Barron and his wife, Shirley Barron. Agents and employees of the Internal Revenue Service failed to follow procedures established for the collection of taxes. Agents and employees of the Internal Revenue Service undertook unwarranted and unauthorized collection activity, made dishonest remarks to the taxpayers concerning the status of the collection action and/or the law governing the collection action, and unreasonably and improperly delayed the collection action despite repeated requests by the taxpayers, or their agents, to bring the collection action to a conclusion. The taxpayers wanted to bring the collection action to a conclusion, because for the three year period 1993 to 1996, the Internal Revenue Service levied against all assets and income of the taxpayers, Bruce E. Barron and Shirley Barron and undertook other activity which made it impossible for the deceased to further conduct his law practice. In short, Bruce and Shirley Barron suffered an unending and extraordinary invasion and disruption of both their personal liberties and their personal and professional lives during the period of the collection action as a result of the reckless, intentional and unlawful conduct of agents and employees of the Internal Revenue Service. At all times pertinent hereto, Donna Greeley was a Revenue Agent with the Internal Revenue Service assigned to the collection case of Bruce and Shirley Barron. Donna Greeley undertook a pattern of collection activity, as hereinafter described, which evidenced her personal disdain for the deceased, her disregard for established collection procedures, law and regulations, and, generally, an intentional, malicious and unlawful course of collection activity which ultimately resulted in the deceased, Bruce E. Barron, taking his own life on August 6, 1996 (suicide note attached hereto as exhibit 1). The Internal Revenue Service and its officers, while being authorized to collect taxes consistent with the laws of the Internal Revenue code, are not authorized to do so contrary to established rules and regulations. Furthermore, agents of the Internal Revenue Service are not authorized to abuse their power and/or utilize the power afforded to them under the law in a discriminatory manner, or otherwise to intentionally harm or treat unfairly any taxpayer. This is precisely what occurred in this case and the Plaintiffs seek damages as a result.

COMPLAINT

The Parties

1. Shirley Barron is an individual citizen of the United States of America, residing at 48 Old Chester Road, East Derry, New Hampshire 03041, which residence is within the District of New Hampshire. She is also the next of kin and widow of Bruce Barron, Esquire who died on August 6, 1996.

2. Shirley Barron is also the Administratrix of the Estate of Bruce E. Barron, (Rockingham, New Hampshire) County Probate Court Docket No. 1996-0984. Bruce E. Barron, Esq., died on August 6, 1996 at Chatham, Commonwealth of Massachusetts. The estate of the deceased is a proper plaintiff under the provisions of New Hampshire law, RSA Chapter 556, and Plaintiff proceeds on behalf of the estate of her late husband under these statutory sections.

3. The Defendant is the United States of America, through employees and officers of the Department of the Treasury, Internal Revenue Service.

4. Donna Greeley was at all times relevant hereto a Revenue Officer of the Internal Revenue Service and was responsible to carry out her duties in good faith and in accordance with the laws, rules and regulations of the United States and the Internal Revenue Service. Upon information and belief, Agent Greeley is currently employed by the IRS within the State of North Carolina.

BACKGROUND, JURISDICTION AND STATUTORY AUTHORITY AS AGAINST UNITED STATES OF AMERICA

5. This is an action by the Plaintiffs against the United States of America acting through the officers and employees of the Department of the Treasury, Internal Revenue Service, alleging unauthorized tax collection activities pursuant to 26 U.S.C. §7433 which resulted in the wrongful death of Bruce Barron, Esquire on August 6, 1996.

6. The United States District Court has jurisdiction over this action under the provisions of 26 U.S.C. §7433(a).

7. The Plaintiffs have properly presented the claims herein to the Internal Revenue Service through its chief, special procedures function, for the District of New Hampshire as set forth in 26 C.F.R. §301.7433-1(e)(1) and (2) as required by 26 U.S.C. §7433(d)(1). (See attached Exhibit 2).

8. Said claims were denied by the Internal Revenue Service by letter dated May 12, 1997. (See attached Exhibit 3).

9. The Plaintiffs have, therefore, exhausted their administrative remedies in compliance with 26 U.S.C. §7433(d)(1).

BACKGROUND, JURISDICTION AND CONSTITUTIONAL AUTHORITY AS AGAINST DEFENDANT DONNA GREELEY

10. This action also includes a claim against one Donna Greeley, who at all pertinent times to this Complaint, was a Revenue Officer of the Internal Revenue Service assigned to the tax collection case of Bruce E. Barron, Esquire and/or Shirley Barron and/or d/b/a The Law Offices of Bruce E. Barron, Esquire.

11. The Fifth Amendment to the United States Constitution guarantees that no person shall be "deprived of life, liberty or property, without due process of law".

12. Plaintiffs bring this claim against Agent Greeley by virtue of the authority articulated by the United States Supreme Court in Bivens v. Six Unknown Federal Narcotics Agents, 403 U.S. 388 91 S.Ct. 1999, 29 L. Ed. 2d. 619 (1971) and Davis v. Passman, 442 U.S. 228, 99 S.Ct. 2264, 60 L.Ed. 2d. 846 (1979) wherein the United States Supreme Court provided an action in damages for constitutional violations by federal officials. Specifically, Plaintiffs' claim that Agent Greeley, under the color of federal law and with the power and authority vested in her by virtue of her status as a Revenue Officer with the Internal Revenue Service, did intentionally and maliciously abuse said power in the form of unauthorized, unwarranted and malicious collection procedures against the aforementioned taxpayers, Bruce E. Barron and Shirley Barron. The actions of Agent Greeley constitute violations of rights guaranteed to Bruce E. Barron and to Shirley Barron under the Fifth Amendment to the United States Constitution.

BRENNAN, CARON, LENEHAN & IACOPINO
85 BROOK STREET, MANCHESTER, NEW HAMPSHIRE 03104
603-668-8300

13. The Court has subject matter of the action against Agent Greeley pursuant to the provisions of 28 U.S.C. §1331.

VENUE

14. Venue is proper in the District of New Hampshire pursuant to 28 U.S.C. §1391.

FACTUAL AVERMENTS

15. In approximately 1993, the Internal Revenue Service commenced collection activity against the deceased, Bruce E. Barron, and, by virtue of their joint tax return, against Plaintiff Shirley Barron.

16. The alleged tax liability was for the years 1986, 1988, 1989, 1991 and 1992, and concerned tax liability of the taxpayers alleged to be in excess of $200,000.00.

17. As early as August 1993, the Barrons discussed with Agent Greeley a possible offer in compromise as authorized by the Internal Revenue Code, 28 U.S.C. § 7122.

18. As set forth in the Internal Revenue manual, "the Service will likely accept an offer in compromise when it is unlikely that the tax liability can be collected in full and the amount offered reasonably reflects collection potential". IRM 57 (10) 1.1(2-26-92).

19. The Barrons were assisted in their offer in compromise by Marilyn Williams, an "enrolled agent" before the Internal Revenue Service.

20. Under the Internal Revenue Service Code, an offer in compromise is available when the taxpayers do not have sufficient assets to pay the full amount of the

BRENNAN, CARON, LENEHAN & IACOPINO
85 BROOK STREET, MANCHESTER, NEW HAMPSHIRE 03104
603-668-8300

outstanding tax liability. In general, the Internal Revenue Service will accept an offer in compromise which is equal to the net worth of the taxpayers.

21. On or about April 19, 1994, the Barrons' offer in compromise was accepted for review by the Internal Revenue Service.

22. On or about May 25, 1995, Agent Greeley prepared a rejection memorandum for the Barrons' offer in compromise.

23. On or about May 30, 1995, the Barrons' offer in compromise is rejected on the recommendation of Agent Greeley.

24. Following the rejection, the Barrons did file an appeal of the Service's rejection and an appeal hearing was held in approximately September, 1995; present at said appeals hearing were IRS Agent, Kenneth Schuman, and agents for the Barrons, Richard Maloney, Esquire, CPA and Marilyn Williams. (Initial documents received by the Plaintiffs as a result of their Freedom of Information Act requests indicated no records of this meeting, however, after a subsequent appeal Schuman's notes of this meeting where produced).

25. At said meeting, Agent Schuman made statements to Mr. Maloney and Ms. Williams to the effect of the following:

(A) That Agent Greeley had engaged in wrongful and improper collection activities;

(B) That he was outraged with the actions of Agent Greeley;

(C) That the offer in compromise was reasonable and should have been accepted under the rules and procedures of the IRS;

(D) That certain important and vital information had not been disclosed to the taxpayers bearing on their pending offer in compromise;

(E) That certain important and vital information had not been forwarded to him from Agent Greeley;

(F) That he would be preparing an acceptance of said offer in compromise in the near future; and

(G) That he would be having a discussion with Agent Greeley "behind closed doors" to address her outrageous and improper collection activities.

26. In reliance on the representations of Agent Schuman that the offer in compromise would be accepted, the taxpayers:

(A) Withdrew a Freedom of Information Act appeal which they had made following the Greeley rejection;

(B) Notified the other creditors that the matter with the IRS had been resolved; and

(C) Became relieved that the long, difficult ordeal with the Internal Revenue Service had come to an end.

(D) By letter dated October 27, 1995, (from Richard J. Maloney to Kenneth Shuman), did confirm and summarize the agreement which had been reached at the September 1995 meeting, and, in reliance on said agreement, did formally withdraw their Freedom of Information Act appeal. (This letter is attached hereto as Exhibit 4. Neither Mr. Shuman nor any other IRS official ever responded to this letter).

27. In approximately January 1996, Richard J. Maloney communicated with Agent Schuman requesting an update on the long pending offer in compromise and the status of the pending appeal.

28. Notwithstanding the statements in the September 1995 meeting and the stated urgency with which this matter needed to be resolved, Agent Schuman and/or other employees/officers of the Internal Revenue Service did fail to respond to and

accept the Barrons' offer in compromise as had been promised at said meeting.

29. In approximately late July/early August 1996, Bruce E. Barron was notified by his primary lending institution, the Pelham Bank & Trust, that it would be foreclosing on the real estate owned by Mr. and Mrs. Barron. Upon Plaintiffs' information and belief, Pelham Bank & Trust undertook this course of action because of Mr. Barron's inability to resolve matters with the IRS.

30. On August 6, 1996, Bruce E. Barron committed suicide at a residence owned by him in Chatham, Massachusetts. In his suicide note (attached as Exhibit 1), the deceased made clear the suicide was the result of the actions of the IRS and the consequential actions of his primary lending institution.

31. Shortly after word of the deceased's suicide, the Internal Revenue Service notified Plaintiff Shirley Barron that the offer in compromise was, by virtue of the suicide, rejected and that they would be seeking to collect the full amount of the tax liability from Shirley Barron. It was the stated intention of the Internal Revenue Service to collect the full alleged tax liability from Bruce Barron's life insurance proceeds. Said life insurance proceeds had been designed and intended to be payable to Plainitff Shirley Barron for her support and the Barrons's sixteen-year-old daughter.

<u>Unlawful Collection Activities of IRS and/or Agent Greeley</u>

32. While the taxpayers' offer in compromise was under consideration by the IRS, the following occurred relative to the collection case of Bruce E. Barron and Shirley Barron:

(A) The IRS, through Agent Donna Greeley, did continue collection activity

BRENNAN, CARON, LENEHAN & IACOPINO
85 BROOK STREET, MANCHESTER, NEW HAMPSHIRE 03104
603-668-8300

notwithstanding the fact that said collection activities were contrary to establish IRS policy;

(B) Agent Greeley became well aware of and discussed with the taxpayers the fact that a bankruptcy filing would eliminate the vast majority of their current tax liability;

(C) Agent Greeley contacted Bruce Barron's elderly mother, a $500.00 creditor of Mr. Barron, while, at the same time, made no remotely comparable inquiry of any other creditor;

(D) Agent Greeley became aware in early 1995 that Mr. Barron was depressed and potentially suicidal on account of the ongoing collection action, yet she made no effort whatsoever to expedite her review or alter her collection activities;

(E) Agent Greeley became aware that the pending IRS action has caused Mrs. Barron extreme psychological harm and loss of sleep;

(F) Agent Greeley made an unlawful levy against Shirley Barron's individual retirement account. In preparing the levy form, Agent Greeley unilaterally and without authorization made a handwritten alteration to an IRS levy form which has specifically exempted such a levy (see copy of altered levy form attached as Exhibit 5); Agent Greeley purported to have such levy form be effective as against Mrs. Barron's IRA account. (In a subsequent memo prepared concerning this collection case [attached as Exhibit 6], IRS Agent Schuman concludes that said levy was done without proper management approval and that the validity of the action was "highly questionable".); The levied IRA funds were ultimately refunded to Mrs. Barron after the death of Bruce Barron without explanation or apology;

(G) Agent Greeley, while continuing to request information in her search for further assets of the taxpayers, never informed the taxpayers that the amount of their offer in compromise was within $2,610.00 of the amount which she had determined to be collectible by the IRS; Agent Greeley made the conscious effort not to notify the taxpayers of this fact, citing purported (and unfounded) noncompliance with "business liabilities". (See rejection memorandum of Donna Greeley dated May 25, 1995, attached as Exhibit 7);

(H) Agent Greeley informed the taxpayers that their offer in compromise must be rejected due to the fact that Mr. Barron had not filed his 1994 tax return while said tax return was under lawful extension, a fact that Agent Greeley was repeatedly informed by the Barrons and their agents;

(I) Agent Greeley informed the Barrons, or their agents, that the offer in compromise could not be accepted because the taxpayers' business liabilities and/or quarterly unemployment taxes were not in compliance; in response to these allegations, Bruce Barron notified Agent Greeley that he was in compliance, supplied evidence that he was in compliance and demanded evidence of the alleged noncompliance; Agent Greeley refused and/or neglected to provide any such information, but nonetheless continued collection activity and maintained her position without any merit or evidence whatsoever;

(J) Agent Greeley made repeated, unauthorized and/or unnecessary requests for information from the taxpayers, which such requests were not authorized by IRS rules nor did they constitute reasonable collection activities by the Department. By way of an example of such a request, Agent Greeley requested the taxpayers' previous six months grocery receipts, which request can under no circumstances be deemed reasonable or warranted under the circumstances;

(K) Agent Greeley informed the taxpayers that their offer in compromise had been submitted for review on several occasions; however, in a May 1995 meeting, it was learned that Agent Greeley had been deceitful to the taxpayers, had never forwarded said offer in compromise for review despite her representations to the contrary, and further informed them that said offer would not be presented for review until all of the unwarranted information which she was requesting was received by her. Prior to this revelation in the May 1995 meeting, Donna Greeley had repeatedly stated that her supervisors were reviewing the offer or that her requests for additional information were demanded by "the powers that be" when, in fact, unbeknownst to the Barrons, no "supervisors" nor "powers that be" had yet received said offer in compromise;

BRENNAN, CARON, LENEHAN & IACOPINO
85 BROOK STREET, MANCHESTER, NEW HAMPSHIRE 03104
603-668-8300

(L) Agent Greeley levied upon the wages of Shirley Barron, an employee of the Town of Londonderry, New Hampshire despite the fact that the taxpayers had offered to pay directly to the IRS all amounts which were subject to the levy. Agent Greeley refused to release said levy to save Mrs. Barron the embarrassment of having the levy against her wages. Agent Greeley also stated to the taxpayers that it would be unlawful for her to release said levy. Said statement was false;

(M) Agent Greeley did make unlawful demands for confidential client records of the law practice of Bruce E. Barron, Esquire; and

(N) Agent Greeley did levy against all incoming receivables and bank accounts of Bruce E. Barron, thereby making it difficult, if not impossible, to continue to conduct business.

33. In an August 23, 1996 memorandum to the file from David A. Hatherly, Associate Chief, Boston Appeals (attached hereto as Exhibit 8), Mr. Hatherly makes reference to "over-zealous" collection activity of Donna Greeley.

COUNT I
AS AGAINST DEFENDANT UNITED STATES OF AMERICA
UNAUTHORIZED COLLECTION ACTIVITIES, 28 USC §7433

34. The Plaintiffs hereby incorporate by reference each and every allegation made in the preceding paragraphs as if fully set forth herein.

35. The actions of the Internal Revenue Service and its agents and employees, including, but not limited to, those activities set forth in the preceding paragraphs, constitute collection activities undertaken with reckless or intentional

disregard of the provisions of Title 26 of the United States code and the regulations promulgated thereunder, including the provisions of the Internal Revenue Manual.

36. The aforementioned collection activities which were undertaken by the Internal Revenue Service and its employees and agents were not designed to enhance collection by the United States Government, but rather were designed to humiliate, embarrass and harass the Plaintiff, Shirley Barron, and the Decedent, Bruce Barron.

37. All of the unlawful collection activities set forth in the preceding paragraphs proximately caused the Decedent, Bruce Barron, Esquire, to take his own life on August 6, 1996 and caused direct economic damages to the Plaintiffs in an amount in excess of the statutory cap set forth in 26 U.S.C. §7433 of One Million Dollars ($1,000,000.00).

COUNT II
AS AGAINST DEFENDANT DONNA GREELEY

38. The Plaintiffs hereby incorporate by reference each and every allegation made in the preceding paragraphs as if fully set forth herein.

39. The aforementioned collection activities of Donna Greeley evidence a vendetta and a "portrait of lawless and arbitrary vendetta fueled by the power of the State", Rutherford v. United States, 702 F.2d. 580 (5th Cir. 1983), for which the Plaintiffs are entitled to compensation for damages caused thereby.

40. In undertaking collection activities against Bruce and Shirley Barron, Agent Greeley had the duty to undertake her responsibilities so as not to offend the Barrons' constitutional right to be free from deprivation of liberty without due process of

BRENNAN, CARON, LENEHAN & IACOPINO
85 BROOK STREET, MANCHESTER, NEW HAMPSHIRE 03104
603-668-8300

law as those rights are articulated in the Fifth Amendment to the United States Constitution.

41. Agent Greeley did not undertake her responsibilities as an IRS Agent fairly or in good faith, but instead utilized the power which she was afforded by virtue of her position to facilitate unlawful, unreasonable and unwarranted collection activities, which in no way assisted the government in its collection efforts, but instead was borne solely out of Agent Greeley's personal dislike for the Decedent, Bruce Barron.

42. As a direct and proximate result of the unlawful actions of Agent Greeley, Bruce and Shirley Barron suffered deprivations of their liberty without due process of law in that: (i) they were forced to endure and accommodate endless unwarranted inquiries and requests for new information by Agent Greeley; (ii) all of their assets, income and receivables were attached and/or seized by Agent Greeley and the IRS, thus causing humiliation and catastrophic disfunction in the personal and business lives of both Bruce and Shirley Barron; (iii) despite their constant efforts to accommodate the inquiries of Agent Greeley, they were forced to endure endless unnecessary delays which were caused by the unwarranted, unlawful, and dishonest conduct of Agent Greeley; (iv) in general, they were forced to endure and suffer extraordinary invasions and disruptions of both their personal liberties and their personal and professional lives as a result of the aforementioned conduct of Agent Greeley.

43. All of the aforementioned conduct by Agent Greeley caused devastating financial and psychological stress and harm to the Barron family which ultimately caused Bruce E. Barron to take his own life on August 6, 1996.

44. As the result of the death of Bruce E. Barron, Plaintiffs have suffered

BRENNAN, CARON, LENEHAN & IACOPINO
85 BROOK STREET, MANCHESTER, NEW HAMPSHIRE 03104
603-668-8300

enormous damages, including, but not limited to, monetary damages, mental anguish, and emotional distress.

COUNT III
BREACH OF ACCEPTED OFFER IN COMPROMISE AND REQUEST FOR SPECIFIC PERFORMANCE AGAINST UNITED STATES

45. Plaintiff incorporates herein by reference each and every allegation made in Paragraphs 1 through 44 of the original Complaint.

46. That on or about April 19, 1994, Decedent Bruce Barron and Plaintiff Shirley Barron submitted an "Offer in Compromise" to the Internal Revenue Service wherein they sought to compromise their tax liability in accordance with the Offer in Compromise procedures set forth in 26 U.S.C. Sec. 7122 and 7121. (The Barrons' Offer in Compromise is hereinafter referred to as the "Offer")

47. The Offer was rejected on the recommendation of Defendant Greeley on or about May 30, 1995. Decedent Bruce Barron and Plaintiff Shirley Barron appealed the rejection of the Offer.

48. On or about September 28, 1995, an Appeal hearing was held before IRS Appeals Officer Kenneth Shuman.

49. As a result of said meeting, Kenneth Shuman agreed to accept the Offer, thus overruling and reversing the rejection of the Offer.

50. Despite his assertions to the contrary following the death of Bruce E. Barron (see attached Exhibit 9), handwritten notes of Revenue Officer Donna Greeley confirm that Kenneth Shuman did, in fact, accept the Offer.

51. Despite the parties' agreement, Agent Shuman and/or other

BRENNAN, CARON, LENEHAN & IACOPINO
85 BROOK STREET, MANCHESTER, NEW HAMPSHIRE 03104
603-668-8300

agents/employees of the IRS failed to complete the necessary formal documentation to finalize the Offer, due to no fault or omission of the Decedent, Bruce E. Barron, or Plaintiff Shirley Barron who complied with all statutory and regulatory requirements for an Offer in Compromise.

52. Following the Appeal hearing, the Barrons and/or their agents, made repeated communications to Agent Shuman, including an October 27, 1995 letter confirming the terms of the settlement (see Exhibit 4 to original complaint), in an effort to finalize the documentation for the accepted Offer and arrange for the payment of the amount due under the Offer.

53. In approximately late July/early August, 1996, Pelham Bank & Trust commenced foreclosure proceedings against real estate owned by the Decedent and Plaintiff. Upon information and belief, Pelham Bank & Trust and/or its successor in interest, First Essex Bank, were unable and/or unwilling to continue to rely on the representations of the Decedent that his Offer in Compromise had, in fact, been accepted by the IRS.

54. Following the death of Bruce E. Barron on August 6, 1996, the IRS, its agents and employees, sought to void their acceptance of the Offer and in doing so, indicated their intention and desire to attach life insurance proceeds which would be available to satisfy the Barrons entire outstanding tax obligation. In short, after accepting the Offer and failing to act thereon, the IRS sought to use the death of Bruce E. Barron as a means to void the Offer in Compromise and obtain said life insurance proceeds.

55. The United States, acting through the IRS, breached the terms of the parties' agreement by its failure to finalize the paperwork necessary to resolve the Offer and by its unilateral failure to honor the terms of the Agreement following the death of Bruce Barron.

56. Estoppel may serve to bar a claim of the Federal Government where there is affirmative misconduct on the part of agents/employees of the United States and reliance on the part of an individual. See, Akbarin v. Immigration and Naturalization Service, 669 F.2d 839 (First Circuit 1982).

57. The actions of agents and employees of the IRS as set forth in the preceding paragraphs constitute "affirmative misconduct" as contemplated by the doctrine of estoppel.

58. The Barrons reasonably relied upon the representations of Agent Shuman that the Offer was accepted, in that they:

(A) Withdrew a Freedom of Information Act appeal which they had made following the Greeley rejection;

(B) Elected to forego their right to file bankruptcy which would have eliminated the vast majority of the Barron's tax liability[1]. (See exhibit 6 to original complaint)

(C) Informed their primary lending institution, Pelham Bank & Trust, that the matter with the IRS had been resolved and that once the final documents were prepared, they would be able to refinance their existing liability with said institution. Upon information and belief, Pelham Bank & Trust

---

[1] The amount of the Barrons' Offer exceeded the amount the IRS would have received if bankruptcy had been filed. If Plaintiff elected to file for bankruptcy today, life insurance proceeds would become a part of the bankruptcy estate. (See Exhibit 6 to Original Complaint).

BRENNAN, CARON, LENEHAN & IACOPINO
85 BROOK STREET, MANCHESTER, NEW HAMPSHIRE 03104
603-668-8300

elected to forego foreclosure proceedings against the Barrons in reliance on the representations that settlement with the IRS had been reached.

(D) In general, became mentally and emotionally relieved that the long, difficult, and emotionally trying ordeal with the Internal Revenue Service had come to an end.

59. While IRS Regulations provide that no offer is deemed to be "accepted" until written notification is received from the IRS, the United States should be estopped from relying on this provision due to the "affirmative misconduct" of IRS agents and employees, the reliance of the Barrons on the actions and representations of the IRS and, generally, the enormous inequities which would result to the Plaintiff if the United States were permitted to rely on this provision to void the acceptance of the Offer.

60. The Plaintiff seeks damages as a result of the aforementioned breach of contract on the part of the United States including, but not limited to compensatory damages, enhanced compensatory damages, interest, attorneys fees, and costs, all of which were foreseeable to the United States at the time the Offer was accepted.

61. In addition and/or in the alternative, Plaintiff seeks to compel specific performance of the agreement between the parties inasmuch as:

(A) A damages remedy would provide inadequate relief to the Plaintiff;

(B) The Plaintiff would suffer an extraordinary injustice if the United States were permitted to renege on its acceptance of the Offer;

(C) The Court could easily supervise and enforce the an order for specific performance.

62. The Court has jurisdiction over this count under 28 U.S.C. Sec. 1331 as it arises under the compromise procedures set forth in 26 U.S.C. Sec. 7122 and 7121.

Jury Demand

63. Plaintiffs demand a Trial by jury.

WHEREFORE, the Plaintiffs respectfully pray:

A. That judgment be entered against the United States of America pursuant to the provisions of 26 U.S.C. §7133;

B. That the Plaintiffs be awarded the statutory maximum damages ($1,000.000.00), along with attorney's fees and costs incurred in bringing this action;

C. That judgment be entered against Agent Donna Greeley;

D. That the Plaintiffs be awarded compensatory damages, punitive damages, attorney's fees and costs incurred in bringing this action against Agent Greeley;

E. The Plaintiff be awarded, as a result of the breach of contract on the part of the United States, compensatory damages, enhanced compensatory damages, interest, attorneys fees, and costs, all of which were foreseeable to the United States at the time the Offer was accepted;

F. The Plaintiff be awarded, in addition to and/or in the alternative, the specific performance of the agreement between the United States and the Plaintiffs which resulted in the compromise and settlement of the tax liability claimed against the Plaintiffs by the United States; and

BRENNAN, CARON, LENEHAN & IACOPINO
85 BROOK STREET, MANCHESTER, NEW HAMPSHIRE 03104

G. That the Court grant such other and further relief as is deemed just and equitable.

Respectfully submitted,
Shirley Barron and Shirley Barron,
in her capacity as Administratrix of
The Estate of Bruce Barron, Esquire
By and through counsel,
BRENNAN, CARON, LENEHAN & IACOPINO

Dated: 9/11/97

By: ______________________
William E. Brennan, Esquire BNH #105
85 Brook Street
Manchester, NH 03104
(603) 668-8300

By: ______________________
Shirley Barron

THE STATE OF NEW HAMPSHIRE
HILLSBOROUGH, SS.

Date: 9/11/97

PERSONALLY APPEARED the above-named, Shirley Barron, known to me or satisfactorily proven to be the person whose name is subscribed to the foregoing instrument and made oath that the foregoing statements made by her are true and correct to the best of her knowledge and belief.

Before me,

____
Justice of the Peace/~~Notary Public~~

Appendix I Complaint, Automobile Negligence

COMMONWEALTH OF MASSACHUSETTS

SUFFOLK, ss

WEST ROXBURY DISTRICT COURT
CIVIL ACTION DOCKET NO.

CHRISTOPHER [redacted], Plaintiff

v.

KAREN [redacted], Defendant

COMPLAINT

INTRODUCTION

This is an action for the purpose of recovering for injuries sustained by the plaintiff, a motorcyclist, when he was forced off the road as a consequence of the negligent operation of a motorvehicle by the defendant.

PARTIES

1. Plaintiff is an individual with a usual address at [redacted] Street, West Roxbury, Massachusetts.

2. Defendant is an individual with a last known address in the Commonwealth of Massachusetts at [redacted] Street, West Roxbury, Massachusetts.

CAUSE OF ACTION

4. On or about June 21, 2003 the defendant so negligently operated a motor vehicle on [redacted] Street in the City of West Roxbury that the plaintiff was forced off the road.

5. .The plaintiff suffered serious injuries and loss of income

6. The plaintiff has been damaged .

Wherefore plaintiff prays this Court award him damages, costs of litigation and such other relief as is deemed appropriate and just.

For the plaintiff,

____

David C. Grossack, Esquire
1320 Centre Street, Suite 103
Hull, MA 02045
617-965-9300
BBO#212890

Dated: June 20, 2006

Appendix J **Complaint - Goods Sold and Delivered**

[J]

COMMONWEALTH OF MASSACHUSETTS

SUFFOLK, SS

ROXBURY DISTRICT COURT
CIVIL ACTION DOCKET NO.

[redacted] CORP.,
Plaintiff

vs.

[redacted] [redacted],
Defendant

COMPLAINT

INTRODUCTION

This is an action for the purpose of recovering a debt for foodstuffs sold and delivered to defendant, a restaurant by plaintiff a wholesale distributor.

PARTIES

1. Plaintiff ("[redacted]") is a business corporation with a usual address at [redacted] Street, Roxbury, Massachusetts.

2. Defendant [redacted] is the owner and operator of a restaurant located at [redacted] Street, [redacted], Massachusetts.

CAUSE OF ACTION

3 On or about [redacted], and on other divers occasions the plaintiff sold and delivered certain foodstuffs to the value of $ [redacted] to the defendant.

4.. The amount of $ [redacted] is due and owing for these items.

5. The defendant has neglected and failed to pay for same.

6. The plaintiff has been damaged thereby.

WHEREFORE plaintiff prays this Court award it damages, costs and interest.

Respectfully submitted,

[redacted], Corp..
By its attorney,

____

David C. Grossack, Esquire
Post Office Box 90
Hull, Massachusetts 02045
BBO No. 212890
Tel: (781) 261-9990
Dated: August 14, 2007

Appendix K Domestic Relations - Request For Production of Documents

[K]

COMMONWEALTH OF MASSACHUSETTS

BRISTOL, ss PROBATE AND FAMILY COURT
DOCKET NO. [redacted]

[redacted], Plaintiff

vs.

[redacted], Defendant

DEFENDANT'S FIRST REQUEST FOR PRODUCTION OF DOCUMENTS

Defendant hereby requests pursuant to Rule 34 of the Domestic Relations Procedural Rules that Plaintiff produce the documents hereinafter described and permit the Defendant and his attorney to inspect them and copy such of them as they may desire.

Defendant requests that the documents be made available for this inspection and copying at the office of his Attorney, David C. Grossack, 1320 Centre Street, Suite 103, Newton, MA 02459, within thirty (30) days of receipt of same.

This request is intended to cover all records and documents in the possession of the Plaintifft, or subject to her custody and control; whether they are located in the Plaintiff's home, principal or secondary office, at the office of her attorney's or any accountant, or at any other place or in the possession of any other person with said records and documents being subject to the Plaintiff's custody and control.

As used in this request, the terms "documents" and "records" shall mean the original, all copies and drafts of all writings of any kind, including, without limiting to the generality of the foregoing, correspondence, memoranda, reports, notes, letters, messages, (including reports, notes, and memoranda of telephone conversations and conferences), calendar and diary entries, contracts, records, data, agreements, checks and canceled checks, check registers, bank statements, brokerage account statements and other designated documents, records, statements and any other designated documents, records, statements or other writings and printed materials specifically referred to in the following numbered requests.

All documents and records specified in each of the numbered paragraphs which follows shall before the period from January 1, 2001 up to and including the date of production of said documents, unless a different date is specified.

1. Copies of the Federal and State income tax returns filed by [redacted] [redacted] individually or jointly, together with accompanying worksheets and supporting vouchers, receipts and all other records substantiating said returns, for each of the years from January 1, 2001 to date.

2. Copies of the Federal and State estimated income tax returns filed by [redacted] [redacted] individually or jointly with Defendant, together with accompanying worksheets, vouchers, receipts, and all other records substantiating said estimated tax returns, for each of the years from January 1, 2001 through the present.

3. Copies of the Federal and State income tax returns together with accompanying worksheets, vouchers, receipts, and all other records substantiating said returns, together with profit and loss statements, for any and all partnerships, corporations, trusts, joint ventures, or corporate or business associations in which you have held any legal or beneficial interest from 1999 to the present date.

4. All records indicating any and all income and gifts received by you or in your behalf from any and all sources during the stated years from January 1, 2001 to date.

5. The registration to all motor vehicles, airplanes or boats currently owned by you or being used by you.

6. Any and all records concerning your employment from January 1, 2001 to the present date, including without limitation, wages, salaries, bonuses, stock options, commissions, earnings, income, employment contracts or agreements, pay raises, promotions, payroll deductions, other deductions of any kind, credit union account, deferred compensation rights, pension plan, pension fund, and other benefits or deductions of any kind which are, were previously, or which may be in the future paid, available, accepted, rejected, credited, offer withheld for any purpose by any individual, agency, department, company or otherwise, or to which you are, were, or may become entitled in the future at any time.

7. All books and records showing any fringe benefits now or previously available to you from any entity which employs you, or in which you have or had a legal or equitable ownership interest, including without limitation, auto expenses, travel expenses, personal living expenses, entertainment expenses, life insurance, bonuses, disability insurance, health, accident and hospital insurance.

8. All documents, records and statements relating to your participation or interest in any retirement investment plan including retirement plans for self-employed persons, pension

plan or profit sharing plan, including without limitation, all applications, confirmations, certificates, policies, beneficiary designations and copies of any such plans.

9. Copies of any original, amended or restated partnership agreement, whether limited or general, in which you now have or had any interest in either as a general or limited partner during the stated years between January 1, 2001 and the date of the production of these documents.

10. Any and all records, statements or documents relating to or having anything to do with any contribution or payment made or to be made by you or in your behalf in money, securities, services or any other form of consideration, to any partnership, whether limited or general, during the stated period from January 1, 2001 to and including the date of the production of these documents.

11. Any and all records, statements or materials relating to any written or oral agreement, contract or understanding between you or in your behalf and any and all partnerships in which you have any interest, separate and apart from any formal partnership agreement, concerning your participation in, relation to, payment or contributions made or to be made by you or in your behalf in money, securities, services or other form of consideration to the partnership, any payments and distributions made or to be made by the partnership to you or in your behalf during the years January 1, 2001 and the present date.

12. Any and all records, documents or memoranda concerning any written or verbal agreement, contract or understanding between you or in your behalf and any partnership in which you have any interest during the stated years relating to or concerning your being able to increase or decrease your partnership interest, and your being able to or having actually withdrawn any capital contribution from the partnership.

13. Copies of all records, financial statements, balance sheets, and income statements received by you or in your behalf and with respect to any and all partnerships, proprietorships, joint ventures, trusts, corporations, or other legal entities, in which you held or now hold a legal or equitable ownership interest, individually or otherwise, during the years specified, including all cash register receipts, canceled checks, financial statements, receipts for inventory, inventory lists and any other document reflecting your income and assets.

14. All records indicating any interest of any kind held by you or in your behalf in any and all corporations, banks or other institutions, foreign or domestic, or any other entities whether or not evidenced by certificates or other instruments during the years specified.

15. All records relating to your ownership of stock options or participation in any stock option plan, in any foreign or domestic corporation or any other entity during the years specified.

16. All records relating to any secured or unsecured personal loan made to your or to any business entity or other person in your behalf during the years specified, whether from a member of your family, a banking institution, or any individual or entity.

17. All records that relate to any secured or unsecured personal loan made to you or in your behalf, during the years specified, whether to a member of your family or to any other individual or entity.

18. Copies of all mortgages, notes receivable or other evidence of indebtedness due you individually, jointly or otherwise, executed to payable, in particular but not limited to your property in Massachusetts, during the years specified.

19. All savings or credit union passbooks or other passbooks of yours, or any card or any other evidence at any savings accounts, credit union account, special notice account, NOW account or equivalent, certificates of deposit, or any other form of deposit, including those held by you, in your name as trustee for another person, during the years specified to the present date, including any such accounts in your name as trustee for another person, during the years to the present date, including any such accounts in your name as custodian for any minor under the Uniform Gift to Minors Act or otherwise for the same period, showing any and all savings, deposits and withdrawals of every kind and nature, and whether or not said accounts or passbooks are now opened or closed.

20. Copies of all records, documents, monthly statements, deposit and withdrawal slips and canceled checks for all savings and checking accounts held in your name, or in your behalf, or in your name jointly with any person or entity, or by some other person or entity for you, or in your name as trustee for another person during the years specified to the present date.

21. Copies of all deeds and records showing any purchase or sale of any real estate in which you held or now hold any interest, whether legal or equitable, either individually, as trustee, or as mortgage, including but without limiting to adjustment sheets showing purchase price and other settlement costs, canceled checks, mortgage, mortgage records and settlement statement, including but not limited to your property in Massachusetts.

22. Any and all records, statements or other evidence showing all payments and contributions in cash or otherwise made by you individually for the acquisition, purchase or construction

of the real property including but not limited to your property in Massachusetts, as described in the paragraph above.

23. Copies of all records, sales agreements and options for the purchase of any real estate or any interest in or related to real estate, including but not limited to, lease, mineral rights, exploration rights, drilling rights, air-space rights, made by you or in your behalf, including but not limited to your property in Massachusetts, from January 1, 2001 up to and including the date of the production of these documents.

24. Copies of all records, sales agreements and options for the purchase of any real estate or any interest in or related to real estate, including but not limited to, leases, mineral rights, exploration rights, drilling rights, air-space rights, or any other similar rights, by you, either in your name, or in your name jointly with any other person in your name, or in your name as guardian for any other person during the stated years.

25. Copies of any and all records, accounts, monthly, quarterly or annual brokerage or other account statements, or other evidences or ownerships, including but not limited to, securities, bonds, mutual funds, other funds of any kind or nature, commodity figures, other figures of any kind or nature, foreign currency, precious gems and metals, gold bullion, treasury notes and bills, municipal securities and bonds, warrants, rights to purchase, puts and calls, annuities, annuities, copyrights, patent rights, trademarks, trademark rights, royalties, rights to trade secrets, any form of tangible rights including any economic rights whether for tax write-off purposes or not, or other investments owned by you individually or held in your behalf, or owned by you jointly with any person or entity, or owned in your behalf with any person, or by you as trustee, or by you as guardian or custodian during the years specified.

26. Copies of any and all records, accounts and statements, including brokerage and other account statements, or other evidence of ownership, indicating or evidencing the dates of purchase and the amounts paid by you for any form of investment during the years specified, including but not limited to, securities, bonds, mutual funds, other funds of any kind or nature, commodity figures, other features of any kind or nature, foreign currency, precious gems or metals, gold bullion, treasury notes and bills, municipal securities and bonds, warrants, rights to purchase, puts and calls, annuities, copyrights, patent rights, trademarks, trade mark rights, royalties, rights to trade secrets, any other form of tangible right including but not limited to any economic rights whether for tax write-off purposes or not, and either owned or registered in your name individually, held or owned by some other person or entity in your behalf, in your name jointly with any other person or in your name in trust for any other person.

27. Copies of any and all records, lists, accounts or statements or other evidences of ownership, indicating or evidencing all investments owned by you, either individually or jointly with any other person or entity, records or statements during the years specified.

28. All records of estates or decedents from which you have received, are receiving or will receive any inheritance or interest in either personal property, real property, other interest or assets, either in trust or otherwise, or monetary assets of any kind during the years specified, or at any time in the future

29. Copies of any declarations of trust, whether revocable or irrevocable, and minute books, if any, for all trusts to which you are a party now or were a party, either as a donor, trustee or beneficiary.

30. Copies of all corporate records, including articles of organization, by-laws and minute books, for every corporation in which you now have, have had, or will have a legal or equitable ownership interest or any other form of interest, during the years specified or at any time in the future.

31. Copies of all records, correspondence, loan applications, and statements of loan accounts, and all records, and evidences of securities and/or collateral pledged therefore, for all loans applied for by you individually, jointly, or in your behalf, whether or not taken or approved, during the stated years, and any related pledge or assignment of any securities for said loans.

32. Copies of any and all personal financial statements prepared by you or by an accountant or by any other person for you or in your behalf in reference to your personal finances or financial status, or for any business in which you have or had any interest during the stated years.

33. Any and all records pertaining to or being evidence of your current outstanding liabilities and indebtedness of any nature or form, including but not limited to any judgments or executions rendered against you in any suits previously pending, the nature and type of suit presently pending in any court whatsoever, and all cases resolved without litigation or which are presently being negotiated.

34. Any and all records, documents, correspondences, writings, memoranda, pleadings, and other materials relating or pertaining to any claim made, suit or legal action brought in your name or in your behalf against another person, firm, corporation or other entity during the years specified.

35. Any and all documents, memoranda, or writings relating to any interest of whatever kind and nature you now have, have had, or may have in real estate, including but not limited to, any interest as owner, co-owner, fiduciary, trust beneficiary (vested or contingent), partner, limited partner, shareholder, joint venture, mortgage, developer, manager or otherwise for the stated years.

36. Copies of all trusts in which you now have, have had, or may have a present or contingent interest, including certificates or other evidences of ownership' if any, indicating such interest, together with copies of all statements, receipts, disbursements, investments, and other transactions related to said trusts during the stated years.

37. Copies of all real estate mortgages held by you or in your behalf or by any entity (including but not limited to realty trusts, partnerships, corporations) in which you now have, have had or may have a present or contingent interest, including but not limited to your property in Massachusetts, during the stated years.

38. Copies of any and all life insurance policies or certificates of life insurance currently or previously in existence insuring your life during the years specified, and any personal disability insurance currently or previously in existence, whether obtained by you personally or by any business or other entity and whether you pay the insurance premiums or the premiums are paid by another individual, a business or other entity, and all such policies on which you or someone in your behalf paid, now pays, or is obligated to pay insurance premiums thereon.

39. Copies of all records, documents or statements showing or evidencing the present or previous cash surrender value of any and all life insurance policies or certificates of life insurance insuring your life currently in existence and on any and all life insurance policies or certificates of life insurance in existence during the stated years.

40. Copies of any and all life insurance policies or certificates of life insurance currently in existence insuring the life of any other person in which you are named at either primary or contingent beneficiary.

41. All credit cards and records of any charge account presently held or utilized by you, either in your name individually or in the name of some other person, business, or business entity, and all statements and receipts received by you in connection with the use of such credit cards and charge accounts, together with a list of all businesses where you are authorized to charge purchases to your account, or to the account of any other person, business or business

entity.

42. All records, statements and receipts for any charge account either in your name individually or in the name of any business or business entity in which you are or were authorized to incur charges for the years specified.

43. Copies of all financial statements, records or documents containing financial information of any nature which have been submitted by you or in your behalf to banks or lending institutions or to any person or business entities in connection with any application by you for credit or loans during the stated years.

44. All records, lists, inventories, appraisals, documents or writings containing a list of all household furniture, furnishings, antiques, stamps, coins, coin collections, silver, works of art, and any other items of unusual of substantial value owned by you individually, in your behalf, or jointly with any other person or entity.

45. All records, documents, receipts and vouchers containing the purchase price of each item of household furniture, furnishings, antiques, stamps, coins, coin collections, silver, works of art, and any other items of unusual or substantial value owned by you individually, in your behalf, or jointly with any person or entity.

46. All records, documents, vouchers and receipts pertaining to the transfer by sale or gift or otherwise of any personal property by you to any other person, business or business entity during the years specified.

47. All records, statements, documents or materials containing any and all information relative to gains and losses realized from the acquisition, purchase, transfer and sale of all securities, bonds, stamps, coins, coin collections, silver, works of art, and any other items of unusual or substantial value and other investments, whether owned by you individually, in your name jointly with any other person or entity, or in your name in trust for any other person during the years specified.

48. All ledgers, books, (Sec. 521) accounts, documents, cash receipt journals, accounts payable ledgers or journals, and all other records and accounts kept or maintained by you (or under your supervision and direction) or your agents or employees in connection with any business or businesses in which you had or now have any interest during the years specified.

49. All records, documents and other materials pertaining to gifts of any kind made by you to any

person, firm, trust, corporation or other business entity during the years specified.

50. Your passport, whether issued to you individually or to you and your husband jointly, and whether or not it is now valid or has expired, for the stated years between January 1, 200 to date.

51. Copies of all financial statements, records or documents containing financial information of any nature which have been submitted by you or by anyone else on behalf of yourself and/or the Defendant to banks or lending institutions or to any persons or business entities in connection with any application for credit or loans from January 1, 2001 to date.

52. All ledgers, books, checks, check registers, checking accounts, accounts, cash receipt journals, accounts receivable ledgers or journals, and all other records and accounts kept or maintained by you (or under your supervision and direction) or your agents or employees in connection with and during the period of marriage.

53. Each and every document which reflects any bills you have paid for third parties.

54. Each and every document which reflects any gifts you have made to third parties.

55. Each and every documents which reflects any loans you have made to third parties.

56. Each and every document reflecting any litigation between you and other parties.

57. Any and all documents reflecting any fact referred to in your Complaint.

By his attorney,

David C. Grossack, Esquire
1320 Centre Street, Suite 103
(617) 965-9300
BBO No. 212890
Date: January 5, 2006

CONSTITUTIONAL BUSINESS

PO BOX 90, Hull, Massachusetts 02045
617-925-5253 • FAX 617-925-3906 • E-MAIL dcg3@ix.netcom.com • INTERNET: http://www.constitution.org/grossack/cjp.htm

A Publication of Citizens' Justice Programs September 1996

SOVEREIGNTY AND JURISDICTION

BY ATTORNEY DAVID C. GROSSACK

Tremendous confusion exists among pro se litigants and constitutional activists concerning the subjects of sovereignty and jurisdiction. The myths are so prevalent that serious damage will be done to the legal rights of many citizens unless they are corrected.

It is a falsehood that an individual and a government can both be sovereign in the same territory at the same time.

Sovereignty is very closely akin to the concept of eminent domain. Let's look at the definition of eminent domain. Black's Law Dictionary defines eminent domain as follows:

"....the right of the state to ....reassert...its dominion over any portion of the soil of the state on account of...the public good."

The reason why a governmental entity has the legal authority to seize property through eminent domain is because it is sovereign. The Fifth Amendment allows "just compensation" but as anybody who has had property confiscated by the state knows, the compensation is usually not very just.

So what is Sovereignty?

Black's Law Dictionary says:

"The supreme, absolute, and uncontrollable power by which any independent state is governed; supreme political authority;"

Sad to report, but governments are sovereign; people are not, unless they become the rulers of their country.

Sovereignty is a concept rooted in international law. Jean Bodin in 1576 formulated the theory of sovereignty as the power of a monarch to formulate all laws without being bound by them! (See Bishop, International Law; Little Brown 1962)

Bodin's theory also concluded that the power of the sovereign "free though it may be from domestic law, remains bound by the divine law, the law nature and the law of nations."

Brierly, in his "Laws of Nations" (142;4th ed. 1949) commented that:

"At the basis of international law lies the notion that a state occupies a definite part of the surface of the earth, within which it normally exercises, subject to the limitations imposed by international law, jurisdiction over persons and things to the exclusion of the jurisdiction of other states. When a state exercises an authority of this kind over a certain territory it is popularly said to have "sovereignty" over the territory...Territorial sovereignty bears an obvious resemblance to ownership in private law..."

Get the picture? Governments own us; they always have since recorded time. They are not bound by their own laws. Why else are federal officials exempt from most civil rights laws? Yes, you must pay taxes; Yes you must have a driver's license. Yes, you must answer census questions. To think otherwise is virtually seditious in the mind of the bureaucrat; and in the context of legal parameters.

The late Don Smith, editor of Writ Wrap once said:

"Jurisdiction is cold, metallic and fits tightly around the wrists."

In fact, jurisdiction relates to situations in which a state may lawfully take action with respect to things, persons and events such as taking physical action to assert its authority, or ascribe the character of legality or illegality to particular actions or events. (See Bishop, ibid)

Russell Weintraub, in his scholarly text "Commentary on the Conflict of Laws" stated that:

"On the basis of raw power, a national state may, on any terms it deem appropriate, authorize its agencies to make adjudications that are binding within that state...

Jurisdiction to adjudicate is exercised when an agency of a state responds to a dispute between individuals or other legally recognized entities for the purpose of making a determination regarding the dispute that is binding within the state on the individuals or entities involved in the dispute."

(See also Restatement Second, Conflict of Laws)

For this reason a judge may be held liable for damages only when he acts beyond the scope of his jurisdiction.

But what is the real message? Is it that jurisdiction grows out of the barrel of a gun? Or is that civilized men and women have to vest power somewhere to settle disputes, to govern a nation and to act as servants of the people to conduct the chores of statecraft? Perhaps the answer is somewhere in between.

The lesson for litigants is to ignore those misleading messages that tell you that you can ignore rules and regulations of governmental entitles by challenging their sovereignty and jurisdiction. These challenges are usually going to be spurious and doomed to failure unless they are plainly acting outside the scope of their legislative authority.

MAKE THE COURTS USER FRIENDLY

BY ATTORNEY DAVID C. GROSSACK

The pro se trend will not be successful unless the courts become more user friendly. They will not become user friendly without prodding. I want to devote this space to telling you how to prod them. In every county, people who are committed to court reform should be organizing and networking to make sure that courts become truly accessible to people without lawyers and that they have meaningful opportunities to be heard, not just assembly line justice where they routinely get shafted.

Here are some concrete steps:

1. Stop focusing on your case alone. Remember that after your case is over the System will be there. If you don't change the System the next time you have a legal problem you'll still be facing the same arbitrary and capricious judicial hacks. For this reason you must change your mental attitude to include a desire to work for a radical overhaul of the courts and the justice system.

2. Find out who the administrator of the regional court system is. Get a group of people together and circulate a petition requesting that the courts be restructured to accommodate pro se litigants. Demand that courts have forms for every kind of legal situation that are easy to fill out and self explanatory and that will not make the citizenry at the mercy of lawyers and mysterious procedural rules.

3. Make sure that you routinely station court watchers in the courtroom if a judge is particularly nasty or despotic. Write letters to the editor if the judge is a louse. If people who live in his or her judicial district are afraid, have somebody do it from outside the district.

4. Use community access cable television. If your community has a community access cable television station, this means you get free access to a TV production facility and free time on television. Create a show around legal reform. Ask judges to come on the show. If people have been badly abused by the Court, shame people by putting the story on television. See if you can get TV cameras into the courtroom, or even camcorders. If you can't, make a stink!

5. Call up talk radio. Have lots of people call the same day if a judge is acting like a tyrant. If necessary, picket the radio station if they won't let you talk about the judges; and by all mean picket the courthouses, the judges home and the homes of lawyers who oppress people.

6. Contact a company called the World's Cheapest Web Page. They provide Internet publicity at the lowest prices ever heard of. Write to Michael Clark, c/o Commercial Directory, PO BOX 1749.

Keaau, Hawaii 96749. Create a web site to expose the system where you live.

7. Are judges elected in your community? Why do some states allow you to vote for who your judges will be and others make them life appointments? Organize to demand that your legislature allow you to vote for who your judges will be, in every single court in the state. Judges who are unelected will be unaccountable and arrogant. Contact you state legislatures and demand that a statute abolishing judicial immunity be enacted. Judges who are immune from lawsuits have a license to be tyrants. Let them get insurance policies like everybody else does, i.e. lawyers, doctors, accountants and dentists.

8. Support the Grossack Amendment. This a proposed piece of national legislation which will make federal judges elected and subject to civil rights lawsuits.

9. Conduct investigations about the business interests of the families of judges and prosecutors and lawyers. Find out where they went to school, where they worked, what they own and who their friends are. Then you'll be able to unravel conspiracies, conflicts of interest and bias.

10. Become educated as to the structure of the courts. Is there one judge with decision making authority who can change policies and procedures throughout the state?

11. Publish or perish. Create a newsletter or newspaper about the legal game in your community. Seek advertisers. Write up stories about bad judges, outrageous cases and proposed legislation. Make it a community project. Keep lawyers and judges out of control positions in the publication, but ask them to contribute articles explaining their side of the story.

12. Keep Citizens Justice Programs informed of what you are doing. Consider sponsoring a pro se skills seminar by David Grossack. This will give people in your organization the ability to understand the mechanics of federal civil rights litigation, civil procedure, and so forth.

13. Become knowledgeable about faxing and E-Mail. Work to build networks of communication with like minded people.

14. Pass out leaflets if you can't publish regularly. Let the System know the people are getting organized and the game is over.

15. Seek out a sympathetic lawyer if you can find one to suggest how the courts can be made user friendly in your community, or at least get some input. There are many kinds of cases which are brought, but only the most serious should really require legal expertise. Gain understanding of the system in order to reform it.

certificates or articles of incorporation, partnership agreements, trust indentures, charters, by-laws, or other corporate, partnership or trust instruments, and all amendments to any of the foregoing, policy statements, manuals, rules regulations, and guides.

4. The term "documents" includes, but is not limited to, communications, financial records and business records, all as defined above, and in addition, reports, books, pamphlets, periodicals, newspapers and magazines and other publications and clippings therefrom, price lists, advertisements, contracts and other agreements and memoranda of understanding, promissory notes, guarantees and other instruments, calendars, diaries, blueprints, papers, notes, memoranda, prints, sketches, indices, tapes, data processing cards, computer printouts and all other writings, drawings, graphs, charts, photographs, phone-records, other data compilations from which information can be obtained and any other tangible item upon which information is recorded or appears.

5. The term "identify", when referring to a person, organization, business or financial institution, means to state the following information:
   a) name,
   b) occupation and title, if any,
   c) relationship to Plaintiff, if any,
   d) residential address, if any, and
   e) business address.

6. The term "identify", when referring to a document, means to state the following information:
   a) the type and nature of the document,
   b) the date of the document,
   c) the author of the document,
   d) the recipient of the document, and
   e) a brief description of the contents of the document.

7. The term "identify", when referring to a communication, means to state the following information:
   a) identify the persons involved in the communication,
   b) the type and nature of the communication,
   c) the date of the communication,
   d) a brief description of the contents of the communications, and
   e) identify all documents evidencing the communication.

www.ingramcontent.com/pod-product-compliance
Lightning Source LLC
LaVergne TN
LVHW080651011026
849160LV00014B/1385
* 9 7 8 0 9 8 5 0 0 4 5 2 1 *